Desire and contradiction

CULTURAL POLITICS

Further titles in preparation

Desire and contradiction
Imperial visions and domestic debates in Victorian literature

Daniel Bivona

MANCHESTER UNIVERSITY PRESS
MANCHESTER and NEW YORK

distributed exclusively in the USA and Canada by ST. MARTIN'S PRESS

Copyright © Daniel Bivona 1990

Published by Manchester University Press
Oxford Road, Manchester M13 9PL, UK
and Room 400, 175 Fifth Avenue,
New York, NY 10010, USA

Distributed exclusively in the USA and Canada
by St. Martin's Press Inc.,
175 Fifth Avenue, New York, NY 10010, USA

British Library cataloguing in publication data
Bivona, Daniel
    Desire and contradiction: imperial visions and domestic debates in Victorian literature.
    1. English literature. Influence of British imperialism: 1837–1945
    I. Title
    820.9008

Library of Congress cataloging in publication data
Bivona, Daniel
    Desire and contradiction: imperial visions and domestic debates in Victorian literature /
    Daniel Bivona
        p. cm. — (Cultural politics)
    Includes bibliographical references.
    ISBN 0-7190-2953-8 — ISBN 0-7190 2954-6 (pbk.)
        1. English literature — 19th century — History and criticism. 2. Politics and literature — ⊂
    Britain — History — 19th century. 3. Imperialism in literature. 4. Colonies in literature.
    I. Title. II. Series.
    PR468.I4985 1990
    820.9'358'09034—dc20   90-5872

ISBN 0 7190 2953 8 hardback
        0 7190 2954 6 paperback

QM LIBRARY
(MILE END)

Typeset in Joanna
by Koinonia Limited, Manchester
Printed in Great Britain
by Bell & Bain Limited, Glasgow

Contents

Preface

The nineteenth century is the century which saw the emergence of Britain as the world's foremost industrial power and its greatest empire. While it has become fashionable to speak of the ripening of an imperialist ideology which fed the expansion of this empire during the period, most contemporary historians or literary critics interested in this topic have tended to confine their considerations to the political and polemical discourse of the period (Palmerston's and Disraeli's speeches, the works of Seeley and Froude, for instance) and to literary works set in the imperial sphere (the works of Haggard, Kipling, Conrad, and so on). While this strategy for containing the imperial experience has produced some very impressive work, it has also tended to cement in place an unnecessary wall, at least in literary studies, between the 'imperial novel' and its opposite number – the 'domestic novel', as some critics have unfortunately termed it. If the imperial experience of the nineteenth century had a truly profound impact on English culture, the 'domestic novel' ought to carry some traces of its cultural imprint.

As recent theoretical work has demonstrated (Hayden White's *Metahistory*, Fredric Jameson's *Political Unconscious*), there is as little a priori justification for the claim that 'literature' cannot engage in 'debates' as there is for the claim that 'arguments' do not 'tell stories'. Given this fact, there is much to be gained in questioning the conventional rhetorical boundaries between 'historical argument' and 'literature' in examining a topic which has a wide literary and historical purview. The discursive representation of British imperialism in the nineteenth and early twentieth centuries is such a topic, and an examination of it gains much when the received modal boundaries are suspended, and certain key literary, polemical, and historical texts are repositioned within a larger domain which has the structure of both a culture-wide 'debate' on the value and causes of imperial expansionism and a cultural metanarrative or mythology which subsumes even many of the critics of empire. The result is a complex discussion of the foundations both of the modern ideology of imperialism and of the critique of that ideology, one which eschews the goal of simple 'coherence' in favour of revealing the contradictions in these discourses, contradictions which, as Derrida reminds, are always symptomatic of the operation of powerful desires. In short, imperialism is not simply either the good or bad conscience of nineteenth-century Britain, but rather, in an important sense, its unconscious, lurking under the surface of a variety of discourses, conditioning the possibilities for emergence of some and precluding others.

This book seeks, then, neither to replicate the efforts of such classic historical studies in this field as those by Koebner, Strachey, and Thornton, nor to re-examine the imperial literary tradition as Green, McClure, and Brantlinger have recently done, but rather to offer a rereading of Victorian culture that considers the important impact of imperialism in a number of domains usually seen as having little to do with it. By juxtaposing texts that have always been associated with the discourse on empire (Disraeli's Tancred, Lawrence's Seven pillars of wisdom, Burton's Pilgrimage to El-Medinah and Mecca, Kipling's Kim, Haggard's She, and Conrad's Heart of darkness and Nostromo) with other works that have not been discussed in an 'imperial' light (Coningsby, Sybil, Alice's adventures in Wonderland, Jude the obscure) I suggest something of the enormous influence the question of empire had on British culture in the nineteenth and early twentieth centuries. In the process, I examine in detail a number of representations of the relationship of knowledge to power, which is the large question opened up by the literary and historical treatments of empire in the period. In other words, I examine a 'debate' occurring within the context of a culture-wide imperialist mentality which is pervasive but also challenged. I hope by this to demonstrate, not only that the question of empire fired the imaginations of a number of important literary figures during the century, exerting influence far beyond its native ground, so to speak, but that the debate in empire cannot be separated from a broader cultural question – the question of how and under what conditions the alien may be appropriated – which both conditions its emergence and supplies the material for argument.[1]

My assumption throughout is necessarily that the discourse on the other is primarily an inadvertent form of self-representation or self-revelation on the part of its producer. Imperialism and the discourses it spawned, in other words, can be seen as having a major role in producing Victorian Britain's own self-understanding. Thus, the

paradox implicit here – writing the 'other' as an act of 'self'-revelation
– reflects the fact that I share this critical assumption prominent in
post-structuralist 'colonial discourse' theory at least since the publication of Edward Said's Orientalism in 1978: that the discourse on the
'other' tells us more about the 'subject' than about the 'object'.

This study begins with Disraeli's political trilogy (Coningsby, Sybil,
and Tancred) for a number of reasons. For one, Disraeli is one of the
chief authors of a nineteenth-century imperialist ideology tailored to
appeal to the middle classes, and these are his principal literary works
in which he first explored the historical themes which form the
intellectual basis for the popular ideology espoused later in his political
speeches. Existing in a modally indeterminate position, partly fiction
and partly political polemic, these novels cry out for treatment as both
literary texts and political argument. Moreover, beginning from the
Hegelian identification of knowledge with appropriation, Disraeli
plots an imperial metanarrative which anticipates various aspects of an
'imperialist' mentality appearing elsewhere in different guises later in
the century: an ideology of race, a myth of historical origins, and a
metahistory. Most importantly, the trilogy foreshadows Disraeli's later
political role as ideologist of Britain's imperial mission by revealing
his tendency, at an early stage of his political career, to take a
'colonialist' view of class relations within England: the conservative
ideology he champions relies heavily on military adventurism and
appeals to patriotism to surmount class tensions for which it has,
finally, no 'cure' to offer, yet the metahistorical ground of Disraeli's
ideology – the myth of the privileged Jewish origins of world history
– is traced by contradictions which are the expression of an ultimately
incoherent 'imperial' desire.

Mid-Victorian England saw the rise to political and intellectual
power of a middle class strongly influenced by the moralism
characteristic of Evangelical and Dissenting Protestantism. Not surprisingly, the growing demand for a 'serious' moral purpose for empire
fittingly conformed to this more general 'tone' of moral earnestness.
However, it is not difficult to understand that such a cultural atmosphere would also generate rebels. In Chapter 2, I examine three works
(Burton's Pilgrimage, Kipling's Kim, and Carroll's Alice) written by
'rebels' of this sort, works which affect an imaginative alliance
between the imperial field and a discourse on 'play' – the Victorian
antithesis to both 'work' and 'moral earnestness'. Although in
dispatching his Tancred to the Middle East for what are meant to

appear to be 'playful' individual motives, Disraeli had already anticipated a prominent literary tradition of 'unmotivated' imperial adventuring, these three works go much further than Disraeli's does towards conceptualizing the entire imperial enterprise as a game or games.

For instance, Burton's *Pilgrimage to El-Medinah and Mecca* (1856) helps to construct a popular image of the Arab world as a place which allows the European to step outside of Victorian culture to adopt a critical perspective on it and its central values of 'work' and 'duty' (as well as the pervasive and suffocating Victorian moralism against which Burton, at any rate, spent a lifetime rebelling). Moreover, with his insight into the ultimately rule-based structure of cultures and his discovery that 'national identity' is constructed on a network of differences, Burton suggests the metaphor of the 'game' as the only available cultural category for naming what culture is. Although he never explicitly draws the ultimately 'anti-imperialist' inference he might have from this – once concede that the only differences between people are the differences in the rules they follow and one has abandoned any claim to superiority founded on an 'essentialist' notion of fundamental 'biological' or 'racial' distinctions – he influences Kipling's later attack on English ethnocentric complacency in *Kim* (1901).

Kipling adopts the metaphor of the 'game' and applies it wholesale to all aspects of cultural life in the vast agglomeration of peoples known as India. Although he is ultimately interested in supplying a new, more sophisticated justification for empire, one which reckons with the levelling effect of conceding that all people follow codes, and must therefore erect the 'Great Game' of imperial management and endow it with Hegelian 'comprehensiveness' – the Game of all Games, the Game without which there would be no religious or philosophical or cultural games – Kipling leaves his readers in an untenable position at the end of the novel, when the larger English connotations of 'juvenility', which cannot, finally, be detached from the notion of 'game', contaminate the 'Great Game' as well, and we as readers find ourselves called upon to celebrate in epic terms what is little more than a schoolboy's prank designed to foil the plans of some notably incompetent spies.

Nevertheless, *Kim* presents an important challenge to the Victorian cultural hierarchy of work over play and to the English ethnocentric complacency which rests on the smug belief that Englishmen are superior to Indians because of their devotion to 'duty'. However, while Kipling challenges English narrowness, he nevertheless reasserts the necessity of British imperial rule. The move to the claim that the blindness that is English ethnocentrism unfits England to rule alien cultures is a move made, not by Kipling, but, surprisingly, by Lewis Carroll in his earlier classic parable of the logic governing cultural imperialism – *Alice's adventures in Wonderland* (1866). By locating his rigidly conventional child-imperialist in a world which is rule-governed but whose rules lie beyond her ken, Carroll offers the century's most dramatic critique of cultural imperialism. Moreover, by demonstrating that Alice's failures of comprehension lead to her attempts to force fit the 'creatures'' behaviour into her own limited categories of understanding, Carroll underscores the necessary alliance between knowledge and power in the imperial field, the failure of understanding and the need to dominate and control which is both consequence and symptom of that failure.

Chapter 3 examines a 'crisis of the civilized' at the end of the Victorian era, one which is in many ways a consequence of Britain's success in the political game of empire. In the post-Darwinian era that is the late nineteenth century, an intellectual fascination with the alien other, fed at least partly by the success of European arms in the imperial field, occasions a crisis in the way England looks at itself. In part, this is an effect of a growing cultural relativism conditioned by the way in which this new 'knowledge' was being appropriated. In reinforcing the popular equation of the 'savage' with the 'child', evolutionary anthropology's 'doctrine of survivals' managed to undermine the primacy of the 'civilized' over the 'primitive' by insisting 'scientifically' on the kinship between the two. It managed to teach this lesson despite its very careful attempts to distance and contain the 'primitive' through the use of the term 'survival'. Focusing my discussion on a few of the works of three key writers of this period (Haggard, Conrad, and Hardy), I trace a growing crisis in the concept of 'civilization' brought about by the attempt to stipulate a relationship between the 'civilized' and the 'primitive' that is simultaneously one of filiation and opposition.

Haggard's solution to the problem raised by cultural relativism is to translate into post-Christian terms the Disraelian myth that the alien field holds secrets that are at base Europe's own: in Haggard, one must return to the primitive world of the present to renew oneself by recapitulating the rise of the 'race' out of primeval barbarism to modern civilization. Civilization, in other words, must re-establish a fruiful relationship with the primitive against which it defines itself: a position which implies the corollary political argument that primitive ways of life should be preserved by a British empire with a self-consciously custodial mission. In *Heart of darkness* Conrad's Marlow, by contrast, enacts a similar return, but one which emphasizes the dangerously solipsistic stakes in such a return to the 'first ages': unlike the Hegelian 'master' Kurtz whose mastery is a form of slavery and whose civilization is largely brutal savagery, Marlow assumes the role of 'proletarian', the motor of history, whose devotion to work keeps him afloat and sufficiently detached from the dirty shore activities to enable him to avoid stepping into the self-referential abyss which is Kurtz's exercise of unchecked power. Marlow's detached engagement expresses both Conrad's thoroughgoing cultural relativism and the ambivalent attitude toward imperialism and European 'civilization' which this engenders: engaged in a 'dirty business' in which the removal of Kurtz is tragically necessary, he nevertheless reserves the right to comment ironically that he has been the witting instrument of a worsening fate, for Kurtz's successor will undoubtedly be worse. Eschewing the role of Hegelian 'master', Marlow cannot purchase the perspective of Hegelian 'Wise Man' either, for Leopold's Congo – like the imperial field generally – is a world of only 'masters' or 'slaves'.

In *Jude*, Hardy produces the century's most thorough critique of the effects of deracination and the failure of historical return to reconstitute a satisfactory relationship between the 'civilized' and the 'primitive'. Jude is the alien within, born into a privileged relationship to the primitive agrarian past of England, but spurned by the representative of English civilization – Christminster – which consistently reimposes the boundary which separates the 'civilized' from the 'primitive'. *Jude the obscure* can then be seen as a parable of the exercise of the imperial power to exclude translated into the terms of social class. Moreover, Jude's own failure to establish a fruitful relationship with his own 'primitive' past marks the degree of his own deracination: like the exiled colonial 'native', he adopts Christminster's method of excluding the past despite the fact that he is himself a 'survival' of that past and victim of the same process of exclusion. Cut off from a fruitful relationship with an agrarian past with its roots in the pre-Christian culture of England and denied entry into the modern 'civilized' England of knowledge and power, Jude becomes the archetype of the modern stateless exile as victim.

Acknowledgements

This project owes a great deal to a number of people who made very helpful suggestions at every stage. I wish especially to thank Herb Sussman, Antonio Feijo, Bennet Schaber, David Cody, Robert Robertson, Claudia Springer, Shormishtha Panja, George Landow, Dore Levy and Patrick Brantlinger for their comments and inspiration. I am grateful to Perry Curtis for directing me to some very useful secondary material and for allowing me to inflict some half-digested ideas on his Literature and Society seminar at Brown University. Above all, thanks go to Robert Scholes and Roger Henkle for helping me get this project off the ground, and for their trenchant comments on my writing.

This book would never have been finished without valuable assistance from the English Department at Rhode Island College and from the Research Foundation at the University of Pennsylvania.

Finally, I wish to thank my wife, Jeannie, and my children, Laura, Michael, and Kathryn, for their help, their understanding, and most of all, their patience.

Disraeli's political trilogy and the antinomic structure of imperial desire

Any account of Britain's 'imperial century' which does not devote some attention to Britain's pre-eminent 'scribbling' MP is sadly deficient in colour if not in intellectual substance. Benjamin Disraeli is often cited as the most important nineteenth-century architect of Britain's imperial ambitions, the cuttingly ironic Parliamentary speaker whose florid oratorical descriptions of the promise that imperial conquest holds influenced a number of young men (and women) of promise to conceive of much of the world as a field for the exercise of their own ambitions. Yet the sample of speeches which is cited in proof of his influence is rather small: in fact, one speech – the justly acclaimed address at the Crystal Palace in 1872 – is often held to stand for a great number of others in which Disraeli purportedly constructed for Britain a vision of a grand imperial future. Contrary to popular expectations, when he was finally given a chance to rule as Prime Minister for an extended period in the 1870s, Disraeli proved himself far more the adroit manipulator of the public symbols of empire than a leader bent on expanding it to geographically impressive dimensions. The crowning of Queen Victoria as Empress of India is the event which tells us most about Disraelian imperialism, although the years 1874-1880 did see the purchase of the Suez Canal, an event with important repercussions in subsequent decades.

Despite the paucity of evidence of Disraeli's overt interest he unquestionably laid the groundwork for a new Tory ideology, one which would discard inherited 'Little England' notions in favour of an enthusiastic embrace of a world-historical mission. This mission Disraeli, more than any other political leader, helped to shape in a direction favourable to imperial expansion: henceforth, stirring appeals to patriotic sentiment would characterize the Tory plan to enlist the political support of the middle and working classes in post-

Reform England. The by now familiar ideological programme by which the working masses are enlisted into jingoist projects as a means of deflecting the impetus for domestic political and social reform was pioneered by Disraeli, who deliberately set out to rebuild the base of Conservative political support to ensure that the party would survive the era of Reform. Because of his success, he not only gave the Tory party a new life (like Bismarck's Chancellorship, Disraeli's Prime Ministership was notable for the introduction of the first extensive social welfare legislation Britain had known: ensuring that it would be seen as a gift from a benevolent, paternalist government rather than as a response to radical agitation by the masses. This programme was enacted in 1875.) but he contributed heavily to shaping the Victorian national temper in a direction ultimately favourable to a more grand idea of 'empire'.[2]

The evidence of Disraeli's interest in the political expediency of imperial visions can be found, not in his early political speeches of the 1830s and 1840s, which are largely devoid of any reference to England's 'imperial mission', but rather in his early literary works – especially the 'political trilogy' of the 1840s (Coningsby, Sybil, and Tancred). There Disraeli fleshed out the themes which set the stage for his later ideological linkage of domestic social and political reform with imperial expansion. Interestingly enough, the publication of these three novels coincided with the greatest Parliamentary successes of his early career: his defeat of Peel over the Corn Law issue and his subsequent recognition as de facto head of the Tory party in the Commons. This 'coincidence' of Disraeli's rise to political pre-eminence and his writing of the three books by which he is chiefly known as a novelist by posterity is, I submit, no coincidence at all but rather a demonstration of the importance of Disraeli's novels in positioning him ideologically on political questions which were 'in the air' in the 1840s. To Disraeli, novel-writing was an expedient act of political ambition which, like the artificially curled hairlock adorning his forehead and the black velvet waistcoat in which he wrapped his form early in his career, called attention to him by setting him visibly apart from the sober squires in the Commons to whose ideological beliefs he had, nevertheless, pledged public allegiance.

Beyond merely marking his difference, however, his novels and especially his 'political trilogy', were written to establish the 'emotional' basis for this new conservative ideology with which he hoped to reinvigorate the Tory Party in the era following the downfall of Peel.

The trilogy offers a wish-fulfilling realignment of political debate: one which resolves, in a fantastically grand (and logically and ideologically suspicious) imperial synthesis, the pressing domestic social question about what role the middle and working classes should play in governing nineteenth-century Britain. In a literary gesture which anticipates the late-century stress on imperialism in the politics of Lord Salisbury and Joseph Chamberlain, Disraeli's trilogy, read as a unit (as Disraeli insisted it should be read), promotes the expansion of England as the inevitable extension of the project of finding a place for the middle and working classes in the governing structure of the country. His novels, in short, gave him a forum in which to undergird domestic political fantasy with imperial fantasy, and to do so in a way which insulated Disraeli the political leader sufficiently from the full implications of this alignment.

The trilogy develops its imperial metanarrative in a characteristically Disraelian way. Disraeli conceives of history as structured like a spiral, permitting progress or displacement forward provided it is conceptualized in terms that evoke the hallowed past.[3] This was a strategy suited to the context of the heated political debates of the late 1830s and early 1840s. While middle-class reformers were expressing vehement displeasure with the failure of the Whig-inspired Reform Bill of 1832 to enfranchise the entire middle class, Chartist mobs in the streets were pressing their demands for an additional widening of the franchise to encompass the working class. A new Tory ideology with staying power would have to address the very insistent reality of the need for domestic political change. How to clothe this necessary change in the garb of ancient English precedent is the project Disraeli sets for himself in the trilogy. Moreover, during a period when England's 'imperial' (the word is anachronistic here) policy was being fashioned in a decentralized way and for baldly private economic and bureaucratic motives – largely by the East India Company, in fact – Disraeli set out, in *Tancred*, to establish a 'moral' and emotional justification for imperial expansion which would clear the way for the late-century celebration of a more public ideal – the 'white man's burden'. However, there were severe limits to how far this political 'bounder' could push the Conservative squires who were the base of his support. Disraeli felt he could only sell the idea of geographical expansion to the 'Little Englanders' if he could justify imperialism as an attempt to restore an ancient unity disrupted in the modern era. In short, as only the trilogy reveals, Disraeli came to see the mission to colonize alien cultures as an imperative of the same form as the mission to 'colonize' the middle and working classes in England. In the trilogy, England's duty is defined as one of expanding by appropriating and reshaping the alien to suit its purposes, under the guise of restoring an ancient unity. Thus, *Tancred*, the final book of the trilogy, an Orientalist lark which Disraeli prized over all his other novels, is also the culmination of the trilogy, for it carries the mission *civilisatrice* of *Coningsby* and *Sybil* beyond the domestic sphere into the imperial field of the Middle East. The Middle East which is remade in the imagination of the would-be crusader Tancred de Montacute is different in degree but not in kind from the aristocratic-dominated utopia which emerges from the ashes of English civilization at the end of *Sybil*.

Disraeli's emphasis on the appropriation of the alien (domestic or foreign) is rooted in a quasi-Hegelian epistemology, a legacy of Romanticism that shaped the thinking of a number of Victorians including Disraeli's contemporary Carlyle. In discussing the 'aims of knowledge' in his *Logic*, Hegel defines the act of 'knowing' as a process of 'taming' or 'domesticating' that which stands outside of, and is therefore opposed to, the subject. As he argues:

The aim of knowledge is to divest the objective world that stands opposed to us of its strangeness, and, as the phrase is, to find ourselves at home in it: which means no more than to trace the objective world back to the notion – to our innermost self.[4]

This reduces to the idea that cognition – knowing – is really a process of 'reappropriation', of discovering the subject in the object, of finding the self in the world outside the self, of reducing the strangeness of what is alien to us by uncovering the reality of its familiarity. As Alan Sandison asserts in *The wheel of empire*:

the development of the Romantic antinomy leads to a moral imperialism, by which is meant literally the expansion and aggrandisement of self, where, in the classic Hegelian manner, the subject wages a continuous war of conquest against the alien object. And the principal weapon is the thoroughly Hegelian one of cognition. (Sandison, p. 61)

This implicitly imperial appropriation of the unfamiliar by the subject-which-knows received perhaps its most influential contemporary formulation in Carlyle's Teufelsdröckh's advice to his reader to 'Feed' on the 'Not-Me' in order to cure the disease of self-consciousness.[5] But it was Nietzsche who, later in the century, was to draw the nastier implications out of this epistemological stance (while also, of course, endorsing them in one sense):

The spirit's power to appropriate the foreign stands revealed in its inclination to assimilate the new to the old, to simplify the manifold, and to overlook or repulse whatever is totally contradictory – just as it involuntarily emphasizes certain features and lines in what is foreign, in every piece of the 'external world', retouching and falsifying the whole to suit itself. Its intent in all this is to incorporate new 'experiences', to file new things in old files – growth, in a word – or, more precisely, the feeling of growth, the feeling of increased power.[6]

Borrowing Nietzsche's terms, then, one can assert that Disraeli's novels thematize 'digestion' and 'growth'. The three novels are tied together by a common thread with imperialist implications: a concern with identifying that which lies outside the subject and which, at least initially, represents a threat to the subject, a threat which is only removed when the non-subject's unfamiliar mask is removed and it is discovered always already to have been a part of the subject. The result of this process is a displacement: the unfamiliar is revealed as familiar and the subject undergoes a displacement (or 'growth' in Nietzsche's sense). In ideological terms, the trilogy embodies Disraeli's political metanarrative, charging England with the mission of incorporating into the polity first the middle classes (in Coningsby), then the working class (in Sybil) and, finally, alien cultures (in Tancred). In this respect, Tancred's imperial setting (in England's 'legitimate sphere of influence') is crucial: when the Montacutes arrive in Jerusalem at the end of that book, they complete a cycle of expansive incorporation initiated in the first book with Coningsby's symbolic merger of the aristocracy and the manufacturing class.

II

Coningsby, the first book of the trilogy, marks the high point of the influence of the neo-feudal 'Young England' movement on Disraeli, and the aristocratic hero of the novel is patterned, in a highly flattering way, after George Smythe, a younger colleague of Disraeli's in the Young England group in the Commons. Coningsby's eventual recovery of his lost inheritance, through a roundabout route, from his grandfather Lord Monmouth and his eventual marriage to Edith Millbank are intended to mark both the metaphorical passage of landed wealth from a decadent Regency aristocracy to a youthful, but serious and reform-minded, Victorian one and, more importantly, a symbolic merger of the manufacturing class with the landed aristocracy: a fantasy empowerment which is presented here as a taming process which softens and civilizes the unpolished manners of the middle classes as it appropriates their world-historical energies.

However, Disraeli attached to the fifth edition of this book (in 1849) a preface of seemingly questionable relevance in which he reminds his English readers of the importance of Asia to Europe. Picking up a theme to which he devotes a great deal of space in many of his novels (as well as in his biography of his political patron Lord George Bentinck), he argues for the importance of recognizing the Jewish origins of the Christian Church. Although a familiar theme with Disraeli, he casts it here in a form intended to shock his readers:

The church is a sacred corporation for the promulgation and maintenance in Europe of certain Asian principles, which, although local in their birth, are of divine origin, and of universal and eternal application.[7]

This passage has a decentring effect on common prejudices: is not Europe the centre of Christianity? Moreover, the term 'Asian', one suspects, like the commonly used term 'Orient', works to deceive by implying a speciously singular referent. Written after the completion of *Tancred* in 1847, this preface suggests a latter-day attempt on Disraeli's part to give renewed emphasis to this theme in the trilogy's first book so as to link it more closely to *Sybil* and *Tancred*, especially to the latter book's projection of Judaism as the privileged origin of Christianity – the 'mother', if you will, of European Christian civilization.

In his insistence on the Jewish origins of Christianity, both in this preface and in each of the books of the trilogy through his mouthpiece Sidonia, Disraeli reveals very clearly an allegiance to essentialist notions of race as well as a commitment to a Burkean account of history as that which softens barbarous behaviour by reminding of the truth which lies at the origin. To assert, for instance, that a Jew was the founder of the Christian Churches of Asia is to refuse the common designation of an early Christian as precisely one who has refused Judaism; yet Disraeli insisted throughout his career on the 'Jewishness' of the Church fathers. To Disraeli, what is conventionally seen as exterior is originally interior and remains so: it is the function of historical knowledge to erase false boundaries, revealing a hidden unity underlying the appearance of diversity.

To argue, as he does here, that a knowledge of the past can itself help to reunify what has been dispersed over the course of time – for a reversal of the *Diaspora* is the key to Disraeli's historical myth – is to run counter to the main impetus of the Romantic notions of history on which he is also relying. For, as Geoffrey Hartman argues, it is the Romantic discovery that a knowledge of history reveals the past existence of 'immediate experience' only at the price of barring the subject from ever re-experiencing it. The Romantic is acutely conscious of the gap between subject and object, man and nature, but only his living in a world characterized by these divisions enables him to glimpse the world of immediate experience from which he is barred.[8] What Disraeli offers, on the other hand, is a wish-fulfilling promise of a 'restoration' of the object to the subject by a reappropriation of the former by the latter, a dissolving of the barriers which divide them through the revelation that the barrier is ephemeral. In this respect, Sidonia's seemingly authoritative claim in *Tancred*, 'All is race', is a disguised oxymoron: the Disraelian notion of 'race', while seeming to suggest a principle of differentiation, merely cloaks an underlying sameness, a sameness revealed to the initiate with a thorough knowledge of history (*Tancred*, XV, p. 191). If one defines 'history' as the serial succession of novelty or difference, one can assert that Disraeli advocates a return to a time before history, before differentiation and dispersal, and advocates it as a lesson which history itself – paradoxically – teaches.[9] The complicated contradictory logic of this position structures all three books of the trilogy; it constitutes a singularly ambivalent thread stitching together his views of empire, his racial theories, and his 'Tory Democratic' interest in justice for the lower and middle classes.

This contradictory logic is precisely what relates Sidonia's 'digressions' on the importance of 'racial purity' to Jews to the dynastic and sexual themes of *Coningsby*. Coningsby is an orphan, yet an orphan blessed with a name for which there is already a matching manorial seat – Coningsby Castle, the home of his grandfather Lord Monmouth. His first visit to Coningsby Castle, thus, is already a return, a return underlined by the familiar greeting he is accorded by the servants when he arrives. Yet this 'return' suggests the key structural pattern of the book: all forays into the unfamiliar are in some sense uncanny returns in this novel. Coningsby's plot is a repetition of his father's in basic form: first embraced and welcomed by the imperious

Monmouth, he later alienates his affections and finds himself disinherited. In fact, it is Millbank (Coningsby's eventual father-in-law, the representative of industrial capitalism in this book) who first explicitly notes the parallels between Coningsby and his natural father when, in rejecting Coningsby's request to marry his daughter Edith, he reminds him that in seeking her hand he would be repeating his father's primal mistake – the error that led to his disinheritance – of choosing a wife from the lower classes. However the words Millbank uses to warn Coningsby ('You are in the same position as your father; you meditate the same act', *Coningsby*, XIII, p. 103) manage to reinforce a suggestion of incest while simultaneously criticizing his planned exogamy. The ambiguity of 'same' here reveals the author's hand intruding to taint Edith who, the novel hints, may well be closely related to Coningsby's mysterious Spanish (Sephardic?) mother.

This incest threat which Disraeli carefully works up behind the scenes of this novel is forecast much earlier in a staged love scene at Coningsby Castle between Villebecque and his titular daughter Flora, the woman who, at her death, leaves the manor to Coningsby in gratitude for his noble behaviour towards her. Although the sugges-tion of incest in this scene turns out to be misleading (we discover, eventually, that Monmouth is Flora's real father), the scene does manage to insinuate that it constitutes the pattern for the other love relationships in the novel. When Coningsby notices what seems to be a portrait of his long-dead mother hanging on the wall of the Millbanks' dining room and later discovers the uncanny resemblance between Edith and his mother (as well as both women's unspecified connection with Spain), his pursuit of Edith for a wife is certainly tainted by what are intended to appear to be incestuous motives.

That Coningsby would seek a replacement for the missing mother he idealizes, and finds her in Edith who resembles her physically, is certainly not an odd plot event given the preoccupation of the Victorian novel generally with incest (or the threat of incest), a preoccupation for which an 'Oedipal' explanation might now account: denied an opportunity of 're-establishing' what is actually an imaginary 'original' relationship with his mother, the boy seeks to master the attendant frustration by establishing a relationship with a new object who resembles her. Thus, marriage is a substitute for life at the breast because of the analogical or metaphorical relationship between the woman one marries and the mother one misses. Leaving aside for a moment the difficulties raised by the fact that the 'mother'

herself is already a substitute,[10] a 'difficulty' which menaces the very
notion of 'origin', and one to which our discussion will return, it is
striking that the resolution of the plot in Coningsby implicitly acknowledges that actual 'restoration' of the 'original' is interdicted: in
Disraeli, 'restoration' requires a displacement in order to achieve
legitimacy. 'Restoration' is the ideological disguise that displacement
or difference must assume.

More importantly, however, Disraeli's attempt to incorporate the
alien under the guise of the original or familiar, while explicable in
terms of psychological motives, also serves a dynastic and political
function, as it did for the upper aristocracy throughout the nineteenth
century. Like the authors of the Old Testament who sought to mediate
between conflicting political demands in constructing their accounts
of the disparate origins of Solomon's wives,[11] Disraeli needs to bestow
an anomalous origin on Edith to render their eventual marriage as
simultaneously endogamous and exogamous: Coningsby needs a wife
drawn from his own class on whose values he can count, as well as
one drawn from the manufacturing class so that his marriage can
function as a symbolic attempt to reinvigorate the tired blood of a
decadent aristocracy (best represented by the dissolute and waspish
Lord Monmouth here). Like Jane Austen's Fanny Price in Mansfield Park,
Edith Millbank is an outsider whose attractiveness lies in her
paradoxical familiarity. As the daughter of Coningsby's erstwhile
father Millbank, the spokesman in this novel for the 'essential
aristocracy' that is the manufacturing class, her merit is guaranteed,
and her brief appearance in Tancred (XV, p. 131) underlines the fact
that she becomes a witty drawing room ornament after marrying
Coningsby. But her resemblance to Coningsby's mother and her
never-fully-explained connection with Sidonia and his privileged site
of origin – Spain – reinforces her dual nature: exotic and 'homey',
alien and familiar, sexualized and innocent, middle class but also –
secretly – aristocratic. Her marriage to Coningsby refounds the
Coningsby line as a more inclusive whole, merging the aristocracy and
trade, Coningsby and Hellingsley, the 'formal' and 'essential' aristoc-
racies.

The duality at the heart of the Victorian Bildungsroman's preoccupation with incest is rather baldly manifest here. The Victorian novel
constitutes itself as a form which offers middle-class readers vicarious
access to the manners of the upper classes, including the custom
among the peerage of consolidating wealth and title through close

intermarriage. However, it also offers a class-based critique of precisely these practices by insinuating that intermarriage be seen as morally degrading, as, in short, incest. The proto-eugenicist argument that goes on under the surface of these Disraelian texts evolves out of a preoccupation with the ambiguous notion of 'good breeding' – anomalously both a process of 'education' under the 'proper' circumstances and a term which refers to the physical act of breeding itself – ambiguous because it represents an experience which is simultaneously the object of middle-class envy and the focus of middle-class resentment as the traditional means by which the peerage consolidated its social privileges. In Disraeli's novels (as well as, especially, in the works of the other members of the 'Silver Fork' school such as Maria Edgeworth and Edward Bulwer-Lytton) representations of the manners of the upper classes are steeped in authorial ambivalence of this sort. Disraeli's lavish descriptions of the various dishes served at his young lord's coming of age offer a related example of this type of overdetermined representation: in these scenes, he manages both to impress his readers with the pageant of aristocratic gourmandizing and to excite their resentment at the typically aristocratic 'waste' that this costly feasting entails.

Coningsby's marriage to Edith, who is associated with a number of heterogeneous historical and psychological elements here – the maternal, the Jews of the *Diaspora*, and the English manufacturing class – brings Coningsby (metonymically 'Young England') into anomalous alliance with world-historical forces which, in Disraeli's imagination, are projections of a privileged and fructifying origin. The plot assumes a spiral shape, as Coningsby's pursuit of the seemingly alien – the prohibited Edith – returns him somehow to the familiar and original – Judaism as the origin of Christianity, the mother he never knew. Yet the origin to which he returns inevitably recedes before him as he removes the mask to reveal it as merely a substitute for an anterior point. For instance, the repetitive structure of his plot which enacts this spiralling movement is mirrored in the parallelism of institutions here: Parliament becomes the public school writ large; hence, Coningsby's ascendancy among the Young England group in the Commons late in the book is but the natural fulfilment of the promise of leadership made by his earlier ascendancy at Eton. In fact, his Parliamentary cohorts – Oswald Millbank, Buckhurst and Henry Sydney – are the same figures who lionized him as a public school boy. The narrator even credits Coningsby's school experience as the origin of the emotional qualities which stand him in such good stead later in his career, while simultaneously denying Eton that privileged role by depicting it as a substitute for a primal experience of tenderness that was denied him:

> The sweet sedulousness of a mother's love, a sister's mystical affection, had not cultivated his early susceptibility. No soft pathos of expression had appealed to his childish ear. He was alone among strangers calmly and coldly kind. It must indeed have been a truly gentle disposition that could have withstood such hard neglect. All that he knew of the power of the softer passions might be found in the fanciful and romantic annals of schoolboy friendship. (*Coningsby*, XII, p. 150)

The 'first great separation of life', as Disraeli's narrator disingenuously terms Coningsby's leaving Eton, is already a substitute, a 'repetition' of an earlier separation from his mother which the novel takes for granted and which it calls on to motivate his search for his mother in Edith Millbank. No sooner does the narrator identify an origin than he denies that origin's 'originality' by marking it as a substitute for one that is always deferred. School here functions like a Derridean 'supplement': an experience both primal and secondary simultaneously, both the source of special feelings which later experiences will recall or repeat and a compensation for a missing primal experience; in fact, an event which falls outside the binary logic of absence and presence although it must be recovered within the terms of this logic.[12] Thus, the narrator treats it as both origin and repetition. In fact, however, origins are never truly originating in Disraeli, whether they are identified with public school values, the maternal, feudal social ties, or the founding principles of the Disraelian brand of Toryism.

Nevertheless, Coningsby's response to Lord Monmouth's request that he stand for Parliament on the Conservative side reiterates Disraeli's need to re-establish something which is worthy of reverence because grounded in an 'original' state of social relations:

> 'Let me see authority once more honoured; a solemn reverence once again the habit of our lives; let me see property acknowledging, as in the old days of faith, that labour is his twin brother, and that the essence of all tenure is the performance of duty; let results such as these be brought about, and let me participate, however feebly in the great fulfilment, and public life then indeed becomes a noble career, and a seat in Parliament an enviable distinction.' (*Coningsby*, XII, p. 139

Not surprisingly, the 'authority' which Coningsby wishes to see re-established here is the authority of 'history', or more accurately, of a peculiar romanticized view of the history of the Middle Ages that characterized the political theology of Young England.[13] One could say that Disraeli is essentially attempting to relegitimize traditional lines of descent and inherited privilege by establishing the need for them to be refounded (or, in Millbank's terms, 'earned') by each new generation. As Young England was founded to repurify and remonarchize the Tory Party, so Coningsby's inheritance of his grandfather's estate through Flora relegitimizes an otherwise traditional (albeit roundabout) chain of inheritance: by receiving the estate as an unasked-for gift from the generous Flora, Coningsby experiences the emotion of gratitude otherwise alien to those who come to riches as a matter of right. Thus, he is placed in a position analogous to that of Eustace Lyle's tenants: suitably humbled by the experience of having received something for which he has not asked and which he has no 'right' to expect. The central mythic problem the book sets out to solve then – how to marry bourgeois ambition and talent to aristocratic legitimacy so that the state can prevent revolution and refound itself as a more inclusive, although still hierarchically-organized whole – is merely one form of a more general, implicitly 'imperialistic', task: how to incorporate the exterior into the interior while legitimizing that incorporation as the merger of two spheres imagined as always already one.

III

Sybil, Or the Two Nations, Disraeli's fictional attempt to come to terms with Chartism and the larger 'Condition of England' question in the early 1840s, hints in its very title that the problem involved in reunifying a class-divided English society stems from the fact that upper and lower classes are separated by a gulf so wide they can be said to live in different nations. As Stephen Morley tells Egremont early on, the two groups live by completely different social rules:

'Two nations; between whom there is no intercourse and no sympathy; who are as ignorant of each other's habits, thoughts, and feelings, as if they were dwellers in different zones, or inhabitants of different planets; who are formed by a different breeding, are fed by a different food, are ordered by different manners, and are not governed by the same laws.' (*Sybil*, XIV, p. 87)

What this passage implies is that any reunification of the two 'nations' will involve the subjection of one to the other, force being the traditional means employed to make independent 'nations' one. However, the romantic medievalism of Young England, which, to a certain extent, still shapes Disraeli's political vision at the time of writing this novel, guarantees that that subjection will be represented as a benevolent one: a new paternalist order much like that of Eustace Lyle's estate, wherein the different and unequal but complementary rights and interests of lord and serf are harmonized. Like the implied new society of which *Coningsby* forecasts the emergence, the new society that the ending of *Sybil* promises will coalesce out of the ashes of ruined Mowbray Manor will be a society that is still hierarchically-organized, still ruled by a landed aristocracy, albeit one which has earned what it has inherited and which has demonstrated through its benevolence its right to rule the masses. *Sybil* sets out initially to demonstrate that England is two nations, only to awaken the reader finally to the same realization as Sybil and Egremont at the end: that the two nations are really one.

Locating the seeds of radical Chartism in the 'unjust' Whig-inspired Reform Act of 1832 (just one of the countless gestures of transparently partisan ideological posturing in which Disraeli engages throughout his novels), Disraeli argues that this legislation nevertheless accomplished one good thing: it encouraged people 'to pry into the beginnings of some social anomalies, which, they found, were not so ancient as they had been led to believe, and which had their origin in causes very different from what they had been educated to credit' (*Sybil*, XIV, p. 44). Thus, the task of the hero in *Sybil* becomes to 'pry into the beginnings', to apply the corrosive test of historical precedence to the social arrangements of the present, in order to determine what is in need of changing. In charging his hero with the task of questioning the 'beginnings' of 'social anomalies', Disraeli means to establish this medievalized ideal as a centre which will ground the process of questioning: henceforth, one questions in order to measure the distance England has fallen from this 'community'; that this 'community' did once exist is not in question. While this project makes the novel unique in its Tory Radical questioning of the early Victorian social order, Disraeli's attempt to arrest the 'questioning' at an arbitrarily chosen point in his idealized Middle Ages reveals the conservative ideologue desperately attempting to sandbag his own radical social criticism, introduced to challenge the bases of class privilege in industrial society, before it floods the edifice of landed wealth.[14]

The gesture Disraeli makes to forestall this erosion of authority is as old as conservatism itself: a version of the 'Great Chain of Being' mythology which justifies class differentiation and hierarchy within human societies because they recapitulate the hierarchical structure of the cosmos. Despite the 'Whiggish' origin of his hero and the association of his family with the despoliation of the Church in the time of Henry VIII (the historical 'crime' to which Disraeli traces the origins of the great Whig fortunes), Egremont, a 'second son' of the nobility, is also described as having an affinity with the sixteenth-century monks whose lands were confiscated at that time as well as with the larger 'yeoman' class to which Disraeli assimilates them. Like the monks of old (themselves mainly 'second sons' of the aristocracy) and the 'squires' of a slightly later time, Egremont is implicitly assigned the task of legitimizing the hierarchization of English social life by demonstrating in his own person that what is wrong with Britain in the nineteenth century is not the fact that it is governed by an aristocracy, but rather, the fact that that aristocracy has wrongheadedly laboured for hundreds of years to abolish the mediating class, to reduce English life to the vicious simplicity of master and slaves. As Sybil's father Gerard tells Egremont:

All agree that the monastics were easy landlords; their rents were low; they granted leases in those days. Their tenants, too, might renew their term before their tenure ran out: so they were men of spirit and property. There were yeomen then, sir: the country was not divided into two classes, masters and slaves; there was some resting place between luxury and misery. (Sybil, XIV, p. 87)

What Disraeli condemns here is not hierarchy or differentiation but simple division in two: a social organization founded on the distinction between the interior and the exterior, a division which turns the lower classes into a restive alien realm, threatening to social peace and upper class privilege. In this sense, the novel promotes social mediation as the principle means of reinforcing the legitimacy of the traditional class structure.

In this respect, Disraeli's representation of the 'Saxon' lower classes in Sybil is governed by a dual purpose: they must appear alien because they have been historically marginalized, and, as such, constitute a threat to the aristocratic 'interior' of English life;[15] but they must also bear the traces of an 'original' interiority which guarantees that they are always already truly English. Both master and slave are interdependent for reasons that Nietzsche underscores: mastery is established only in opposition to slavery; the master is 'essentially' nothing more than he who subjugates (*Beyond good and evil*, p. 215). Thus, the 'Norman' aristocracy which Egremont represents is dependent on its opposition to the 'Saxon' lower classes for its very self-definition. However, the consequences of this view – one close to the views of the most extreme Chartists in the novel – are insupportable to Disraeli because they would strip away the civilized veneer covering aristocratic authority, revealing it as but the pure exercise of power for its own sake – a consequence that would eventually threaten the exercise of that authority. Thus, in staging a metaphorical marriage of upper and lower classes through the love affair of Sybil and Egremont (although even this is anomalous, as Sybil, we later discover, is a dispossessed aristocrat), that is, in having these lovers rise above the Norman/Saxon opposition, Disraeli must locate them in a seemingly new but really old mediating class – the yeoman class. There is an unintended irony then in Egremont's passionately attempting to dispel the mists of democracy that cloud Sybil's judgement, at one point, by chasing them with some new Disraelian mists of his own – the 'new generation', implicitly a revival of the yeoman class in Victorian England:

'The people are not strong; the people never can be strong. Their attempts at self-vindication will end only in their suffering and confusion. It is civilisation that has effected, that is effecting, this change. It is that increased knowledge of themselves that teaches the educated their social duties. There is a dayspring in the history of this nation, which perhaps those only who are on the mountain tops can as yet recognise. You deem you are in darkness, and I see a dawn. The new generation of the aristocracy of England are not tyrants, not oppressors, Sybil, as you persist in believing. Their hearts are open to the responsibility of their position. But the work that is before them is no holiday-work. It is not the fever of superficial impulse that can remove the deep-fixed barriers of centuries of ignorance and crime. Enough that their sympathies are awakened; time and thought will bring the rest. They are the natural leaders of the people, Sybil; believe me, they are the only ones.' (*Sybil*, XIV, pp. 400-1)

The mystifying function of the 'new generation' is nowhere better revealed than here. Not only does Egremont reaffirm the Disraelian doctrine of the inevitability of hierarchy, but he unequivocally rejects the claim that the activities of the Chartist lower classes can be an actual stimulus to the reformation of English political life. The 'new

generation' cannot be shaped by the opposition of a 'Saxon multitude'; it is self-defined, and will change with its own 'increased
knowledge of' itself. Although intended to mark a promise that Saxon
slavery will soon end, this claim to self-sufficiency of a new master
class is enabled only by the deployment of a new (but really time-
worn) opposition: the opposition of 'civilization' and 'barbarism',
which informs the first four lines of Egremont's speech. Henceforth,
the goal of the 'new generation' must be to restore the exteriorized
'Saxon' multitude to the interior of English political and social life, but
such a gesture cannot dispense with the opposition of exterior and
interior. Thus, the lower classes must retain a threatening aspect that,
in Disraeli's view, justifies the continuation of aristocratic political
privilege and authority. The invasion of Mowbray Manor at the close
of the novel, then, not only justifies Egremont's 'yeoman' rescue
mission as a mission to save civilization from the threat of barbarian
hordes (as, parallel to this, Disraeli's depiction of the social hierarchy
of 'Bishop' Hatton's mob both parodies the English class structure and
drives home the ideological point that hierarchy – and rule by either
the best or the worst – is a human universal), but it precipitates a new
symbolic 'sorting out' of exterior from interior, barbarian from
civilized, the truly alien from those who only temporarily appear so,
'Bishop' Hatton from Dandy Mick. The storming of Mowbray Manor
at the end of the book can then be read as a purification rite meant
to separate those who were always already truly English from those
who are tarred with foreign associations. Thus, although the rioters
evoke the home-grown rebellions of English history, from Wat Tyler
and the Levellers to the Luddites, this riot is led by a man of undeniably
'heathenish' antecedents, a point Disraeli conveys by describing the
burning castle as the 'funeral pyre of the children of Woden' (*Sybil*,
XV, p. 184) and having the 'Liberator' strut the stage as a grotesque
but unmistakable parody of Napoleon returned from Elba.[16]

The book ends with Disraeli's offering a wish-fulfilling resolution
to an essentially irresolvable social and psychological contradiction.
Egremont's putting the truly unassimilable members of 'Bishop'
Hatton's mob to the sword metaphorically purifies the lower classes,
rendering the remainder fit for assuming their rightful if lowly place
in English society – at the cost of his repeating the historical crime by
which the usurping Norman crosses the Channel to enslave the
original Saxon. And, the marriage which symbolizes the new incorporation of the working classes into the mainstream of English life –

the union of Egremont and Sybil – is rendered anomalous by Disraeli's revelation of Sybil's secret aristocratic lineage. The tension between the imperative to incorporate the alien – the exogamous necessity – and the contrary demand for racial and class purity – the endogamous ideal – the tension which is left unresolved in Coningsby, remains likewise to fissure Sybil. The social critique which Disraeli initiates in Sybil, the project of returning to origins to question the foundation of the present, leads Disraeli to pursue an origin whose authority evaporates as he invokes it. Ultimately, the quest to affect a political synthesis of upper and lower classes under the guise of a restoration of a medieval moment founders where all such schemes must founder: one cannot both privilege an arbitrary point of origin and, simultaneously, promulgate the doctrine that a knowledge of history will offer knowledge of that origin. Historical precedence is corrosive of all authority; history never offers a centre without undermining its centrality.

What becomes clear by the end of Sybil is that Disraeli really has nowhere to go but in the direction of further literalization of his romantic historical schemes. Where the ancient Hebrew race serves as an analogy for the construction of a vital English aristocracy in Coningsby, Sybil traces a nineteenth-century class conflict which is not so much analogous to earlier conflicts as it is the actual fruit of unresolved social class tensions persisting from the sixteenth century and earlier. Thus, the notion of Roman Catholicism as completed Judaism, the idea for which the 'Norman' vicar Aubrey St. Lys is the spokesman, is introduced to sanctify the role of the Roman Church as the centre of a medievalizing dream in Sybil.[17] This religious theme of Sybil, which serves a relatively minor novelistic function here, nevertheless links the book with Tancred and thus prepares its readers for Tancred's 'spiritual' quest to restore 'direct' communication with the divine in the only land where such a restoration is said to be possible – the Middle East. Not surprisingly, miscegenation and religio-imperial appropriation become the overt goals of English aristocratic youth in the final novel of the trilogy. The pursuit of an absolute origin must draw one back, eventually, to the site where history began and to the deed – simultaneously incestuous and exogamous – that lies at the origin of human history, viewed genetically.

IV

Tancred, or the new crusade, published in 1847, has been described by
Philip Guedalla as the 'strangest book ever written on the front
bench'.[18] Written during the years 1845 and 1846, and thus after
Disraeli's successful Parliamentary rebellion against Peel over the Corn
Law issue, Tancred has been thought by a number of critics to be an
attempt by Disraeli to place some distance between himself (now one
of the leaders of the Conservative Party) and his former allies in the
Young England movement (which had, in effect, already died an
unremarked death anyway). Certainly, Tancred's repudiation of the
value of a career in Parliament in favour of adventure in the Middle
East is hardly the kind of sentiment one expects from a leader of the
Conservative Party in the Commons. Yet, for all its exotic strangeness,
its foreign setting and romantic quest structure make it a compara-
tively 'safe' vehicle for the expression of Disraeli's imperial myth at
a crucial turning point in his career.

Tancred is the culmination of Disraeli's trilogy. By transporting his
surprisingly passive aristocratic hero away from his overly-close
English family, depositing him in the imperial field of the Middle East,
and finally restoring his family to him at Jerusalem at the end of the
narrative, Disraeli once again performs the literary conjuror's trick of
confronting the alien, unmasking it to reveal it as familiar, taming it,
and finally displacing 'England' in the process. When the Duke and
Duchess of Montacute move to the Middle East, the final step in the
process of incorporation and displacement has occurred. Henceforth,
for reasons that Tancred implies, England's sphere of political operation,
its field for the exercise of its aspirations, will be in the East; the thrust
of English political energies must be directed outward geographically
(although the actual pursuit of such an enterprise threatens a loss of
'racial purity', ultimately a gradual erasure of the difference which
distinguishes Christian from Jew, aristocrat from commoner, Englishman from foreigner).

For Tancred is a Disraelian hero in many ways like Coningsby. He
comes of age at a time when young men of his class were channelled
into Parliament, but he resists (although more forcefully and
successfully than Coningsby). He meets Sidonia and is impressed with
his ideas on the Hebraeo-Christian Church, finally adopting him as his
most important mentor. However, unlike Coningsby's, Tancred's plot
life does not conform neatly to the model of the progressive spiral.

Where Coningsby's plot begins in lack (of home and mother) and ends in his having to accept metaphorical substitutes associated with those original objects of desire, Tancred's plot life begins not in lack but in what looks like satisfaction. The Montacutes doted on him. As Disraeli says,

From the moment of his birth, the very existence of his parents seemed identified with his welfare. The duke and his wife mutually assumed to each other a secondary position, in comparison with that occupied by their offspring. From the hour of his birth to the moment when this history opens, and when he was about to complete his majority, never had such solicitude been lavished on human being as had been continuously devoted to the life of the young Lord Montacute. (*Tancred*, XV, p. 22)

Indeed, so solicitous are the parents that they even arrange for Tancred to marry his first cousin Kate – an exact parallel to their own situation, for the Duke and Duchess are themselves first cousins. Moreover, as the Duchess does not hesitate to remind Tancred, this arrangement will involve a virtually painless renunciation on his part: 'She is my perfect image, my very self . . . in disposition, as well as face and form' (*Tancred*, XV, p. 33). Thus, Disraeli begins the novel by suggesting a psychological situation just the opposite of Coningsby's: Tancred's plot could be an almost perfect circle: the Oedipal boy who must renounce the mother is provided by his parents with a substitute who is virtually identical; marriage is not a painful imposition of difference but a delightful return of the same.

In rejecting both his parents' marriage plans for him and his father's wish that he enter Parliament, Tancred reinforces the novel's suggestion that parents and son have a relationship almost close enough to be called a *ménage à trois* : 'we should for a time separate' (*Tancred*, XV, p. 63). *Tancred*, in fact, is about the generation of desire out of satisfaction, and thus, provides the key to the imperial metanarrative of the trilogy. To seek a need for Tancred to explore the Middle East one need go no further than to look at his satisfaction: Tancred's motive exceeds the alternative of presence and absence, satisfaction and lack.[19] In rejecting his parents' marriage plans for him, Tancred seeks to escape the cyclical return of the same in favour of an irruption into history and the play of difference. That he casts his plans in terms of a repetition of his ancestor's crusade, however, suggests that he must discover an ancient claim of right in the foreign field, that the alien world is assimilable only under the guise of a reappropriation or reclaiming of what is always already his own, ultimately, that the alien world holds secrets that are at base his own.

In this sense, this *Bildungsroman* looks forward to what amounts to a Victorian novelistic tradition of 'unmotivated' imperial adventuring. The notion that the individual who makes a 'career' of the East does so for reasons that are not, fundamentally, comprehensible within a logic structured along a matrix of absence and presence served an important ideological function in the nineteenth century. Its ideological function is obvious: it procures for the imperialist a certain innocence of intention as well as affording him the option to claim highminded motives. Although some later writers who made use of this structure – Conrad and Kipling come to mind – are also given to examining it critically (for all his nonchalance about having undertaken his riverboat pilot's job, Marlow in *Heart of darkness* is the immediate cause of the removal of Kurtz and his replacement by a company official who will undoubtedly be more venal), it served an insidiously ideological function for many precisely because it authorized the claim that imperial adventurism is somehow nobler when 'freely' chosen, or, as in the case of Haggard and Buchan, that imperial adventuring is really a form of boyish play (this issue is explored at greater length in Chapter 2).

Like the past that has never been present in *Sybil* – the moment when Church, poor, and nobility were one – the privileged moment of the past which Tancred seeks to repeat – the moment when his crusading ancestor Tancred de Montacute experienced his 'direct' communication with God – is, at least initially, intended to function as a centre grounding the play of repetitions here. However, it is quickly superseded by two more ancient 'moments', the creation and the promised redemption of the human race as revealed in Genesis and the New Testament. As Tancred explains to his startled father:

'When I remember that the Creator, since light sprang out of darkness, has deigned to reveal Himself to His creature only in one land, that in that land He assumed a manly form, and met a human death, I feel persuaded that the country sanctified by such intercourse and such events must be endowed with marvellous and peculiar qualities, which man may not in all ages be competent to penetrate, but which, nevertheless, at all times exercise an irresistible influence upon his destiny. It is these qualities that many times drew Europe to Asia during the middle centuries. Our castle has before this sent forth a De Montacute to Palestine. For three days and three nights he knelt at the tomb of his Redeemer. Six centuries and more have elapsed since that great enterprise. It is time to restore and renovate our communications with the Most High. I, by the Holy hills and sacred groves of Jerusalem, would relieve my spirit from the bale that bows it down; would lift up my voice to heaven, and ask, What is duty, and what is faith? What ought I to do, and what ought I to believe?' (*Tancred*, XV, p. 70)

Given Disraeli's historical premises, Tancred's pursuit of the historical original draws him necessarily to the Jews, the originary race, and to a 'moment' necessarily anterior to the medieval moment of the Crusades – the beginnings of human history as revealed in Genesis. Tancred's quest ultimately becomes a quest to arrest and recapture, mythically, the original ontogenetic and phylogenetic moments, for these 'moments' are called into being by Disraeli's diachronic premises – the dynastic assumption that the beginning of a 'line' is the beginning of a history as well as the genetic assumption that human history must have been initiated in an original moment of sexual congress between aboriginal parents. Disraeli's genetic view-point presupposes a beginning point to human history, an Adam to fertilize an Eve who is also, somehow, his sister-self. In many ways, one can see this as a recapitulation of Disraeli's already familiar romantic pursuit of the mystery of diversity: how does unity produce diversity or difference? how can the one generate the many? Both of these questions are already implicitly raised by the 'supplementary' nature of Tancred's imperial quest: how can satisfaction or repletion generate lack or desire?

Thus, when Tancred experiences his crucial 'vision' on Mount Sinai, the incident which energizes his mission, he is charged by the angel with restoring a state of unity, a unity of all the gods – necessarily a unity of cultures as well as a collapsing of a chain of metonymies into a unitary 'experience'. As the angel informs him:

'The equality of man can only be accomplished by the sovereignty of God. The longing for fraternity can never be satisfied but under the sway of a common father. The relations between Jehovah and his creatures can be neither too numerous nor too near. In the increased distance between God and man have grown up all those developments that have made life mournful. Cease, then, to seek in a vain philosophy the solution of the social problem that perplexes you. Announce the sublime and solacing doctrine of theocratic equality.' (*Tancred*, XVI, p. 158)

This pronouncement forecasts the pattern for Tancred's subsequent adventures: he is to embark on a syncretizing mission that is also an historical and personal return. Hence, when Sheikh Amelek sees him off with the traditional farewell – 'There is but one God' – he seals his mission as one to prove the truth of that Arab greeting. The rest of the book will see Tancred sampling, Rasselas-style, the representative cultures of the Middle East, a passage which is really a mythic return through the ages of time back to the absolute point of historical origin, identified here as a Jewish one. Tancred also undergoes, parallel to this, a concomitant psychological return, capped by his reunion with his family in Jerusalem on the last page of the novel. The impulse, of course, behind this desire to restore a once-existent unity – both a political one and a personal or psychological one; in fact, an attempt to bridge the gap between the personal and the political – is the dream of restoring 'presence', the absolute presence of God to man, the closing of the gap between subject and object, signifier and signified, in a gesture which will abolish language, difference, history, and politics. However, the dream of restoring 'immediate' communication is the dream of abolishing communication. The notion of returning through history to a time before history is itself an anti-historical notion. The fantasy of reunifying the races of humanity in a theologico-imperial synthesis is ultimately a fantasy of abolishing the distinction between ruler and ruled, a distinction which is, nevertheless, affirmed elsewhere by Disraeli, as we have already seen, as the necessary precondition for such a reunification. Moreover, the dream of abolishing the interior/exterior dichotomy by uncovering the exterior as always already interior is the dream of obliterating all distinctions, including that between the metaphorical and the literal.

The rest of the novel, then, takes Tancred to three significant places: to the patriarchal 'totem feast' of Fakredeen's Canobia, where he enjoys a lordly banquet in a passage meant to be read as a recapitulation of his own coming of age in England, described early in the novel; to the lost Greek theocratic matriarchy of the Ansarey, where he not only proves his mettle in battle with the Turks but must fight off the sexual temptation of the Queen-goddess to preserve his knightly virginity; and, finally, back to Jerusalem, where he first passes a night of portentous dreams which merge all the important female characters in his life, and then visits Eva the Rose of Sharon in her garden at Bethany to propose marriage to her.[20] Tancred's final adventures trace a familiar if confusing Disraelian pattern that is the expression of a highly ambivalent imperial desire.

Returning at the end of the novel to a Jerusalem which has now become his home, Tancred passes a night of 'agitating dreams': he imagines himself in a Bellamont castle ruled by Fakredeen and, when he 'rushed forward to embrace his mother, she assumed the form of the Syrian goddess, and yet the face was the face of Eva' (*Tancred*, XVI, p. 409). The dream sequence reinforces the repetitive structure of Tancred's plot: not only is Fakredeen's Lebanese palace a recapitulation of his home Bellamont (as Canobia's politics, with more than a little forcing, recapitulate English Parliamentary politics), but, more importantly, the available but undesirable Astarte (the Queen-goddess of the Ansarey, a people Disraeli presumably thought descended originally from Hellenized Phoenicians) is imaginatively merged with the interdicted but desirable mother as well as with the enigmatic and racially interdicted – although not legally prohibited – Eva. When Tancred 'returns' to the 'Garden' at Bethany to confront Eva with the full extent of his passion for her, the Sidonian ideal of 'desert purity', the practice of which, Tancred claims, is the anomalous key to regeneration, is threatened with suspension in favour of his desire for sexual congress with the other half of humanity, represented here by the mother of all – Eva. The claim that barrenness and sexual abstinence are the source of fertility, the renunciatory Sidonian ideal which imposes an impossible psychological burden, is implicitly abandoned in Tancred's gesture toward Eva, although Disraeli the author has too great a stake in it to surrender it at this point.[21]

When the Duke and Duchess of Bellamont arrive at Jerusalem, interrupting and suspending for all time the moment when Eva would have either to accept or to reject Tancred's suit in the garden at Bethany, the scene has been set. Tancred's suit for the heart of Eva – the historical original by virtue of her privileged link with the chosen people and a name which identifies her with the mother of the human race – is interrupted by the arrival of his mother – the psychological original. The once unified 'woman', shattered into a number of shards in a primeval Diaspora, had been provisionally reconstituted into a momentary psychological whole in Tancred's dream through the momentary suspension of interdictions. However, the abrupt rhetorical jolt that the subsequent announcement of the Bellamonts' arrival engenders (the servant's announcement is the final sentence of the text) is occasioned by the fact that outside of the dream is the reality of fragmentation and interdiction: placing the two women in physical proximity occasions a reversal of the historically 'primal scene' with which Disraeli plays – Adam and 'Eva' as (suddenly) children interrupted in the act by the parents. One could say that the humour introduced by the awkward intrusion of Tancred's parents at just this point springs from the fact that they constitute an unwelcome reminder of the fact that Adam and Eve are not supposed to have parents, that, in other words, to 'begin again' is impossible because one cannot discard history in order to renew it.

Disraeli is thus left in a quandary occasioned by his insistence on closing the cycle of Tancred's life by reuniting him with his parents in the East – implicitly, by his attempt to displace England in an East which was to have been already domesticated and prepared for their arrival and assumption of power. Although the imperial metanarrative of the trilogy, the historical dynamic for which Sidonia is the mouthpiece, requires that 'England' be displaced in the East to enact the incorporative gesture which will revivify its own civilization with the world-historical energies of the privileged Jewish race, the ending of *Tancred* abruptly throws into relief the contradictions which ground such a hope through the medium of what has been called Disraeli's 'undecidable tone'. If miscegenation (and empire) is a gesture of cultural reinvigoration and revitalization – if the marriage of Eva and Tancred is to inaugurate a theologico-imperial merger of creeds and cultures – then it must take place regardless of the fact that it undermines the very Sidonian idea of racial and class purity which is offered to Tancred as a model for the English aristocracy to follow. However, Tancred's suit for Eva's hand is also child's play here – a flirtation with miscegenation, a game of 'naughty' children – and this interpretation reinstitutes the renunciatory Sidonian ideal at the cost of calling the 'seriousness' of most of Tancred's adventure into question. That Disraeli is dangling both of these incompatible interpretive possibilities in front of his readers is clear from the abrupt ending and the tone throughout. Disraeli finally offers us the choice of either taking him seriously or treating the entire novel as a harmless *jeu d'esprit*.

Ultimately, this justly famous 'undecidable tone' is but the literary expression of an ambivalent imperial desire which informs all three books of the trilogy. The political implications of such a dual vision must have been clear to Disraeli on some level: thus, the 'undecidable tone' and the exotic setting of *Tancred* – ostensibly removing it from any direct relation to the hot political issues being debated in Parliament in the mid 1840s – suggest an attempt by Disraeli to distance himself from the thematic material, to achieve what American bureaucrats in the late twentieth century would call 'plausible deniability'. Ironically, however, it is precisely this distancing gesture which places this novel in the centre of any discussion of the psychology of imperialism. As Tancred's Jerusalem dreams blend exotic and familiar in a soup which is notable for its suspension of psychological interdictions – domesticating the exotic while sexually charging the familiar and interdicted – so the imperial mission, conceived as a process of reducing the strangeness of the alien by appropriating it to English categories and English political desires, ultimately, subjecting it to the dictates of English political will, runs head-on into the rock of its own incoherence: the East made available for imperial appropriation is inevitably made 'too' available, inevitably remodelled on the lines of an original which never was originating but which nevertheless still bears the signs of interdiction – both a spur to desire and a sign of the impossibility of satisfaction and complete assimilation.

V

While *Tancred's* lines of literary affiliation run backwards to the Oriental Gothic of Beckford and ahead to the Ethnological Romance of such writers as Haggard and Ballantyne, this novel also serves the important literary-political function of locating orientalist fantasy in something resembling an actual Middle East whose politics are being appropriated to English political categories.[22] Disraeli's resituation of the devices of the political novel which he pioneered in *Coningsby* in his depiction of Fakredeen's Lebanon makes it difficult to marginalize *Tancred* as quaint orientalist fantasy. Moreover, *Tancred's* sexualization of the Middle East anticipates Haggard's later inflation of 'Darkest Africa' into a recumbent, inviting female body, awaiting penetration by the phallic hero as imperial adventurer: phallocentric ethnological fantasy set likewise in an actual geographic locale which is the locus of real British imperial desire in the late nineteenth century. Surprisingly the sexualization of the Middle East does not seem to have bothered his more devoutly religious Victorian readers. The overlay of Christian religiosity seems to have seduced even as pious an Evangelical as Isabel Arundell, the well-born wife of the Victorian explorer Richard Burton, who was apparently so moved by the tale that she claimed it inspired her to redouble her political efforts to procure for her husband the British consulship in Damascus.[23]

Ultimately, however, Disraeli wished his readers to see *Tancred* as the culmination of the political trilogy, the work that lends purpose and direction to the whole project, in a manner consistent with its Hegelian premises. This is the sense in which we have read it here. The importance of all three books of the trilogy is their projection of imperial myths in a form in which their fissures become manifest. What counts for critics of Disraeli as 'failures' of art are more often than not ideological inconsistencies stemming directly from the metahistorical projections of Disraeli's imperial desire. The trilogy is an especially ambitious effort to resituate early Victorian discourses on social class, 'race', and history within an overarching ideological framework which is imperialist at bottom. The Hegelian epistemological assumptions which govern the attempt to appropriate the alien in the nineteenth century are deployed in this novel in such a way as to produce symptomatic anomalies: the perpetual 'rediscovery' that the alien was always already familiar and/or family constitutes the ideological substructure of these texts, a substructure which raises a number of cultural anxieties characteristic of Victorian ideology.

For example, Disraeli's trilogy constitutes a heavily fissured discourse on the Victorian umbrella concept 'race'. While in many ways highly conventional in their early Victorian assumptions, Disraeli's own ideas on race are nevertheless interesting because of Disraeli's seeming immunity from the fear of self-contradiction.

If one may generalize about so large a topic, the term 'race' meant roughly 'lineage' in England until about 1800.[24] However, German Romanticism was fashioning a new notion of 'race', one closer to the modern meaning of 'nationality', which was eventually to influence English thought through Romantic science and philosophy. One major figure in this change was Herder, who, in reaction against French Enlightenment notions of universal rationality, coined the term *Volksgeist* to identify the mysterious essences which distinguish different nationalities and 'rationalities'. Simultaneously, the late eighteenth-century discovery of the resemblances between Sanskrit and ancient Greek and Latin by the English orientalist William Jones gave birth to Comparative Philology and its enabling concept of the language 'family'. In the work of the German philologists who developed the implications of Jones' discovery, men such as Schlegel, Bopp and the Grimms, Comparative Philology sought to trace wherever possible affinities among the various language groups in the world in the hope of being able to track the diversity of the present back to some putative primeval unity. In this sense, Comparative Philology was a double-edged intellectual weapon. It was used both to initiate a new way of thinking about human cultures; human history could now be conceived in migrational terms, in which a sequence of peoples originating in a primitive Aryan homeland had spread out across the face of Europe. In this sense, it was implicitly monogenist in tendency. Yet it also led to a re-emphasis on racial essences, especially later in the nineteenth century as the discovery of other major language families unrelated to the Indo-European led philologists (Renan's discovery of 'Semitic' is a classic example) to conceptually freeze the major language families in a position of absolute and unbridgeable difference from one another.[25] This later tendency was consistent with polygenist assumptions about the origins of mankind and contributed inevitably to some of the more insidious forms of Victorian racialism.

In England, the 1840s was a period in which these competing racial paradigms contended with one another for primacy. The older notion of 'race' as 'lineage' persisted, appearing in various guises not only in Disraeli's novels, but in the work of his contemporaries such as Bulwer-Lytton (see The last of the barons, J. M. Kemble, The Saxons in England, and even Thomas Carlyle, Past and present). Meanwhile, the monogenist position on race had become the guiding paradigm of the new science of ethnology. When the 'father of ethnology' James Cowles Pritchard published his Researches in 1848, he identified the 'ethnological problem' as one of demonstrating the unity of mankind – a non-racist project from its inception (Stocking, p. 50). However, a much less generous position was simultaneously being staked out by such polygenists as Robert Knox whose The races of men (1850) argued for the absolute nature of distinct racial essences. Sidonia's claim 'All is race' is strikingly consistent with Knox's articulation of this position.

Disraeli's literary works are striking for the way in which they amalgamate these antithetical positions in an unholy synthesis. His emphasis on the Jews as the originary race is a way of tipping his hat to notions of racialist essence while, through his metamyth, he commits himself to contrary monogenist assumptions about the origin of human cultures. Because the monogenist and polygenist positions are logically incompatible, the novels founder on the rocks of incoherence, as we have already demonstrated. However, Disraeli's linkage of class with race is also quite interesting because it procures for his novels a broader mythic sweep by abolishing distinctions which would normally prevent one from seeing, for instance, domestic class conflict as a clash of distinct races in many respects

foreign to one another. Moreover, Disraeli's toying with miscegenation, however tinged it is with his own personal ambivalence,
undermines the very ideological foundation for racial separation in the
same gesture which reasserts the necessity of it. One can see in Disraeli
more clearly than in other contemporary writers a very complicated
process by which 'racialist' ideas provide the 'intellectual' support for
notions of aristocratic privilege (cf. Gobineau's Essay, 1856) while an
incompatible monogenist metamyth undergirds the ideological promotion of imperial expansionism. To say that these elements in his
novels articulate culturally overdetermined positions in the early
Victorian era is putting the case mildly.

Ultimately, the significance of Disraeli's novels lies in the fact that
they open up critical questions for Britain's nineteenth-century
experiment with 'knowing' and 'shaping' the alien world, while
suggesting that that alien world can be found always already at home,
in fact, that the alien world derives its significance from the fact that
it can be appropriated using the categories of the known in order to
cast light on the unknown dwelling within. Tancred's imperial quest,
because it is described in terms that make it seem 'unmotivated',
'playful' in the English sense of an activity which is set in opposition
to 'work' and 'moral seriousness', anticipates a Victorian discourse on
empire and play, the subject of Chapter 2. Moreover, Disraeli's pre-
Darwinian concern with Middle Eastern cultures which, he asserts,
have persisted unchanged from the beginnings of time, anticipates the
late-Victorian preoccupation with 'survivals' of the past persisting in
the present, an interest of those English writers most heavily
influenced by the discoveries of later Evolutionary Anthropology (the
subject of Chapter 3).

In political terms, Disraeli's Tancred looks forward to a later English
obsession with the Middle East as its sphere of political influence, an
interest which he, more than any other Victorian political leader,
helped to define when, as Prime Minister in 1876, he bought the
newly-dug Suez Canal, instantly investing the Middle East with new
geopolitical meaning as 'the road to India'. Where Victorian travellers
prior to 1876 experienced the Middle East as culturally alien although
tantalizingly assimilable (See Alexander Kinglake, Eothen, 1844, Eliot
Warburton, The crescent and the cross, 1844, Sir Richard Burton, A Pilgrimage
to El-Medinah and Mecca, 1856), the late Victorian traveller Charles
Doughty moves through and helps to reshape a world which is clearly
part of the English sphere of interest. Interestingly, though, it is

Doughty's disciple in the twentieth century, the politically enigmatic T. E. Lawrence, who most resembles Disraeli's Tancred in his dedication to a fundamentally redemptive mission; in his infatuation with the desert as a place of cultural, religious, and ethical regeneration; and in his cultural and historical syncretism deployed in the interest of an ideal that is suspiciously Western – nationalism. Indeed, as the self-appointed prophet of Arab nationalism, Lawrence himself very closely resembles Disraeli the Romantic ideologist in his insistence that nations are built on the fundamentally irrational basis of emotional commitment. Moreover, as an outsider within British society (an illegitimate son of a profligate Irish baronet), Lawrence shared with Disraeli (a man of Jewish extraction who claimed he was descended of Spanish aristocratic forebears who were originally Sephardic) a peculiarly similar commitment to self-fashioning as well as an ec-centric relationship to British power which both nevertheless served so well.

Although *Seven pillars of wisdom* purports to be non-fiction, it is in one sense constructed very much as a Victorian *Bildungsroman*, with a providential plot detailing the gradual emergence of a rather obscure 'orphan' to prominence at the centre of a world-historical event – the British-assisted Arab rebellion against the Turkish empire during World War I.[26] Where Disraeli's *Tancred* enacts a plot traced by the tension between the two seemingly incompatible alternatives of knightly self-abnegation and patriarchal sexuality, Lawrence adopts only the austere Sidonian course. Thus, not only is the book devoid of female characters, but the 'desert', Sidonia's privileged site of 'spiritual' values, is seen as the defining characteristic of the Arab which Lawrence seeks to become. For this reason, his claim 'Semites had no half-tones in their register of vision' functions both as anthropological description and as prescription for Lawrence himself to live the truth of. When at one point during a campaign, he finds himself forced to execute a murderer named Hamed to prevent a blood feud between two Bedouin tribes, Lawrence is steeling himself emotionally to accept just such a philosophy without 'half-tones' (Lawrence, p. 182). This affects eventually his notion of cultural identity, making him incapable finally of maintaining the charade of a dual political role. He takes Damascus in the name of Feisal, although he knows that his ambitions for Arab nationhood have already been secretly repudiated by England and France through the Sykes-Picot agreement: incapable in the end of blending British and Arab identities, he adheres rigidly to one or the other in an oscillation which implies that culture has no half-tones either. The inability to reconcile Middle East and England while retaining an English identity is one of the main reasons Disraeli breaks off the narrative of *Tancred* at the moment when Tancred's parents arrive in the Holy Land.

What is most interesting, though, about Lawrence's initiation into manhood under the pressures of war is the prophetic role it leads him to adopt, for it is just such a role that constitutes 'manhood' for Tancred. Where Tancred's military victory over the Turks on behalf of the Ansarey becomes ultimately just another picaresque adventure, of limited importance in the novel when weighed against his more important role as cultural and religious prophet, even Lawrence comes to the realization that the military aspects of the guerrilla war in which he is engaged are secondary in importance to the project of forming an Arab nationalist consciousness. Thus, Lawrence reproaches himself early in the book for not realizing that 'Feisal's preaching was victory and the fighting a delusion' (Lawrence, p. 173). Ultimately, this leads, in a direction consistent with the Hegelian premises of the operation, to Lawrence's realizing the idea of Arab nationalism in himself. He describes his part as a 'synthetic' one: 'I combined their loose showers of sparks into a firm flame: transformed their series of unrelated incidents into a conscious operation' (Lawrence, p. 216). The intrusive 'I' of much of the narrative must be seen as that of the secular prophet, the prophet of Arab nationalism. The key word here is 'conscious', for it suggests the Idealist metaphysics lurking behind the Lawrentian notion of 'nationhood'. 'Arabia' must be conceived – first in the mind of Lawrence its prophet – before it can achieve world-historical reality.

However, despite the pose Lawrence adopts as Hegelian 'Wise Man', Lawrence participates in a 'slavish' passivity that is secular rather than religious as was Tancred's. Where Tancred attempts to submit himself to God by becoming his instrument to affect a religio-imperial synthesis, Lawrence serves two secular 'masters' – Feisal and Allenby (cf. Lawrence, p. 386). Although he traces this ideal of 'happy slavery' to Arab cultural roots, part of the role he must play as 'Lawrence of Arabia', it clearly serves an important psychological function for him – explaining, not only his 'abasement' before Allenby (and, less so, before Feisal), but his elevating this abasement to the status of ideal of conduct in a world without god, a world in which political masters have taken his place.[27]

Thus, Lawrence's self-reproaches increase later in the book as he gradually grows disenchanted with his dual role. His perception that he is fraudulently playing the Arab nationalist is made more keen as Allenby and the English cause claim a larger share of his allegiance. The latter half of the book, in fact, is marked by rhetorically excessive tributes to Allenby which form a stark contrast to the measured respect he accords Feisal in the first half. One suspects his own need to abase himself before a Master to whom he can throw his life directs him more and more to Allenby as Allenby's military successes in Palestine multiply. In fact, this self-abasement takes a very sensual turn after the capture of Damascus when he says: 'I might let my limbs relax in this dreamlike confidence and decision and kindness which were Allenby' (p. 659). Despite his profession of allegiance to the dream of Arab nationhood in the Epilogue ('the new Asia which time was inexorably bringing upon us', p. 661) and his activities promoting Arab nationhood at the time of the Versailles Treaty, Lawrence knows on some level that his activities on behalf of the Arabs during the war are part of an imperial strategy that his sensual attachment to the strategic 'Master' Allenby makes significant, that the world-historical significance of Arab rebellion lies in its role as Allenby's 'right flank'. Ultimately, Lawrence's oscillation between master of Arab nationality and slave to English political objectives marks him as a twentieth-century Tancred living in Kipling's world, a world from which god has departed but whose place has been filled by English power.

However, with the mention of Kipling we get ahead of ourselves, for Kipling plays a very important role in the construction of a new relationship to the alien which both reasserts the necessity of English rule while reserving the right to critique English ethnocentrism of the Disraelian sort. For that discussion, we must turn to Chapter 2.

The field of play
in the game of empire

In the political realm, it is Disraeli the Member of Parliament who is most often credited with helping to formulate a popular nineteenth-century imperialist ideology capable of compelling the allegiance of the middle-classes (Thornton, p. xiii). His 'romantic' view of the majesty of power allowed him to formulate in words what others were only capable of harbouring in silence. As a later generation of socialist leaders were to be alarmed by the popular appeal of nationalist and imperialist sentiment to the working classes called to battle by their countries during World War I, so the Cobdenites of the mid-Victorian era, committed to the notion that middle-class prosperity was tied to world-wide free trade unencumbered by the demands of ruling a world empire, were dismayed by the political success of Disraeli's emotional appeal to his middle-class listeners to embrace gladly the awesome burden of ruling just such an empire.[1] In part, one can account for this as the fulfilment of the design that motivates his rhetorical strategy in one of his most important speeches; the 'Crystal Palace' speech of 1872 formulates these responsibilities in a way calculated to encourage his hearers to link the fate of empire to their own belief in the worth of individual initiative. As he proclaims, the time is at hand when,

England will have to decide between national and cosmopolitan principles. The issue is not a mean one. It is whether you will be content to be a comfortable England, modelled and moulded upon continental principles and meeting in due course an inevitable fate, or whether you will be a great country – an Imperial country – a country where you sons, when they rise, rise to paramount positions, and obtain not merely the esteem of their countrymen, but command the respect of the world.[2]

One can easily read out of this not only a traditional aristocratic contempt for a set of values that are purely 'commercial' and 'self-serving', but also a conjuring into existence of a 'higher duty', or, at least, a 'higher significance', that necessarily, so Disraeli implies, attaches itself to actions of world-historical importance. Disraeli here is tapping into a surprisingly rich vein of bourgeois dissatisfaction with the values of the marketplace. In uniting familiar middle-class goals with traditional imperialist aspirations, Disraeli is attempting to forge a tenuous alliance that he undoubtedly hoped would help to promote a belief in the worth of empire among a class whose beliefs were traditionally tied, not only to the 'free trade' notions current among the Cobdenites, the group he called 'the Manchester School', but more generally to a life of 'commerce', which in some nineteenth-century eyes, inevitably bound it to the 'little world'. In this respect, Disraeli is one of the legion of empire-promoters in the nineteenth century to insist on the ethical significance of conquest, yet simulta-neously, as Thornton argues, the only major political figure of the mid-Victorian age to be able to 'get away with' a redemptive 'roman-tic' view of the majesty of power wielded for the sake of the powerful – a 'missionary' view that has been turned on its head and stripped of its Livingstonian moral baggage.[3] If empire has anything like a 'moral' purpose, in Disraeli's view, it serves such a purpose for England, rather than for the people of her colonies.

The disjunction that Disraeli's prescription presupposes and pur-ports to heal is that between what one might loosely call a 'bourgeois' set of values (acquisitive, energetic, revolutionary in its initial stages, but ultimately individualistic and narrowly materialistic) and an 'aristocratic' one (grounded in a romantic notion of England as a traditionally 'great' country bound to exercise that greatness on the world stage, sometimes at the cost of blood shed in what is nevertheless held to be an inherently 'noble' cause). Needless to say, this disjunction can operate as an irresistible temptation to modern-day critics wishing to simplify the Victorian debate on empire by casting it as a contest for supremacy between an 'aristo-military' mentality and a 'bourgeois' mentality.[4] Although Disraeli assumes the discursive existence of such a dichotomy, he does so for rhetorical purposes. Even a cursory look at the complex debate over the role of economic factors in encouraging England's imperial expansion in the late nineteenth and early twentieth centuries, a debate initiated by the Victorians themselves, raises grave questions about the usefulness of any analysis which insists on erecting a rigid wall between 'bourgeois' and 'aristo-military' values.[5] Conrad's novels, for instance, perpetually contest this distinction, especially *Heart of darkness*, which is about commercial predation in the imperial field, and *Nostromo*, which challenges the materialist/idealist opposition grounding the metaphorical function of money and 'silver' and, consequently, questions the received cultural distinction between a 'noble martial self-sacrificial' ethos and a bourgeois 'materialist' one.

In any event, as Thornton demonstrates, the institution of the empire effectively barred most attempts to dismantle it until after World War II because of the way in which it was able to press its critics into the service of promoting it. For example, the Cobdenite dream of 'free trade' inevitably required the extension of imperial control to areas of the world newly forced to experience some of its 'benefits', for 'free trade' requires a revolutionary remaking of traditional societies as its prerequisite. And the Scottish missionary-explorer David Livingstone's concern for the natives of Africa, most evident in his attempts to put an end to the slave trade, implied the extension of white rule as an inevitable corollary to his pious wish to bring the benefits of 'commerce and Christianity' to the natives (Thornton, p. 15). Moreover, in the late-century atmosphere of ferocious European imperial competition, the most appealing moral arguments for protecting indigenous people often required the extension of formal institutions of imperial control (Thornton, p. 76).

Thus, Disraeli's attempt to see the imperial field as a new ground for the exercise of bourgeois interests is merely one more expression of the interconnectedness of home and empire in nineteenth-century England. Ultimately, in his Crystal Palace speech, Disraeli holds out the promise that English actions might acquire a significance missing in the everyday bustle of commercial life, a significance guaranteed by success in the game of imperial competition. However, missing from the speech is, not surprisingly, the worldly, 'undecidable tone' that undermines the credibility of Tancred's 'romantic' faith, encouraging the readers of that novel to interpret it as a harmless, juvenile, *jeu d'esprit*. Disraeli is ostensibly attempting to infuse political acts here with a purpose – a motive presumably acceptable to his middle-class public – which contrasts sharply with the ultimately 'motiveless' romantic enterprise of his youthful hero Tancred. Yet, even so, that 'purpose' has a suspiciously hollow ring to it. For one, Disraeli recommends the imperial field as but a useful employment agency for bourgeois youth. Moreover, the ultimate goal of such employment is held to be pure recognition for its own sake ('a country where your sons, when they rise, rise to paramount positions, and obtain not merely the esteem of their countrymen, but command the respect of the world'). No ultimate end beyond recognition itself is proffered. While no one would ever mistake Disraeli for the highly 'moral' Livingstone, nevertheless, a certain almost playful 'motivelessness' akin to Tancred's seems to contaminate even this political vision which, in all other respects, appears to have been carefully tailored to appeal to the English middle-class taste for a moral rationalization for imperialism.

However, one ought not to be surprised that Disraeli the political figure bears some resemblance to Disraeli the author of *Tancred*. In fact, the record of his political career reveals that he was always uncomfortable with attempts to moralize about foreign policy. That he found the Evangelical piety of the English middle-class difficult to fathom he demonstrated on more than one occasion during his career, perhaps no more infamously than in the latter years of his Prime Ministership, when he underestimated the popular appeal of Gladstone's moralistic 'Midlothian' campaign against his pro-Turkish foreign policy.[6]

One might venture the claim that Disraeli's outlook on empire (in *Tancred*) as a playing field for English aspirations, a realm for the exercise of power uninhibited by utilitarian considerations, is a peculiarly 'aristocratically playful' view: as Huizinga asserts, the noble class of many countries has often arrogated to itself (however wrongfully) the exclusive right to irony and playfulness; in part, to emphasize the distinction between itself and the lower classes whose members all too often lead lives of unrelieved and sobering drudgery.[7] And certainly this notion that imperialism might be viewed as a 'game' to be played for the sake of play is not alien to the imaginative literature of empire. For all the sober moralizing of R. M. Ballantyne and Harriet Martineau, the novels of such later ardent imperialists as H. Rider Haggard and John Buchan are still ruled primarily by the 'spirit of adventure'. Moreover, even such 'classics' of imperial-era travel literature as Sir Richard Burton's *A pilgrimage to El-Medinah and Mecca* and Charles Doughty's *Travels in Arabia Deserta* reveal their authors' almost 'childish' delight in exploration, disguise, and the penetration of mysteries that lurk behind the veil of cultural boundaries. Both Burton and Doughty dilate at length on the intricate ceremonies of disguise each must perform in order to lift the veil of secrecy covering Arab culture, to fill in the white 'blot' on European maps that is Arabia (as Burton characterizes his objective). And, of course, English literature's most famous imperialist – Rudyard Kipling – is also one of its greatest celebrators of juvenility, having left a legacy of work (especially *Stalky and co.*, *The jungle book*, 'The man who would be king', and, most

importantly, Kim) which challenges received hierarchical orderings of
the serious over the non-serious, work over play, and utilitarian over
non-utilitarian motives – dichotomies on which all Western moral-
isms (as well as the distinctions between the 'adult' and the 'childlike')
ultimately rest.

On the one hand, one can easily detect a familiar 'serious' purpose
lurking behind the ostensible 'purposelessness' which informs some
imperial literature. Undoubtedly the theme of empire assumed a
privileged place in the growing boys' literature of the nineteenth
century because the emphasis on daring adventure appealed to
children, while, no doubt, the teaching of patriotic virtue had some
appeal for their parents.

On the other hand, my argument goes beyond this. The suggestion
that this 'imperial' literary tradition contests the distinction between
'play' and 'work' or the 'serious' and the 'non-serious' implies that
it serves a compensatory social function in a nineteenth-century
England coming to be ruled by a sober middle-class. Disraeli's
'undecidable tone' in his novels, an expression if ever there was one
of Huizinga's 'play spirit', can thus be seen as an early manifestation
of a phenomenon which was, in a roundabout way, to press empire
as an imaginative adventure into the service of 'domestic' social needs:
empire is also a privileged realm of play, a play denied an outlet in
the English workplace; when all is said and done, it must be admitted
that the individual often engages in imperial adventure for motives that
transcend utilitarian or even moral or religious purposes. Although the
universality of this work/play distinction will be called into question
here (while the necessity of deploying it is nonetheless acknowledged), it is important to note that those writers who were most
interested in collapsing the rigid dichotomy and who used the
imperial field as a privileged site for questioning the work/play
hierarchy (writers such as Disraeli, Burton, and Kipling), nevertheless
all begin with the assumption that they are addressing a sober British
audience for whom the realm of play and the realm of work seldom
interpenetrate.[8]

II

In the nineteenth-century literature of empire, a relatively detailed
representation of the strange customs of alien peoples was a common

feature that helped contribute to the popularity of these works among English readers. A fascination with the exotic was an important feature of English popular cultural life, especially during the latter half of the century, and this literary taste was gladly met by writers whose 'ethnographic' adventure tales were much in vogue.[9] The enormous popularity of such works as *King Solomon's mines* (1885), which Haggard supposedly wrote in six weeks to win a bet with his brother, has possibly as much to do with the almost sympathetic treatment of different black African cultures in it as it does with the English taste for exciting, bloody adventure.[10] As Brian Street demonstrates in *The savage in literature*, English readers enjoyed being fed a diet of alien customs provided those customs could be seen in a light which preserved a treasured sense of moral, religious, political, and racial superiority.[11] However, a few writers (Haggard is one) developed a more 'relativistic' outlook on the primitive by cultivating a perspective that granted some value to 'savage' ways of life, a point of view that surprisingly seldom threatened the popularity of their books. Rather than accentuating cultural differences with the alien in order to baldly congratulate Englishmen on their superiority, the effect of these more 'relativistic' treatments of foreign customs and social rules was to emphasize either the commonality of human kind or to express an overvaluation of the prelapsarian 'savage'. In Haggard's case, for example, a respect for the African 'noble savage' is in direct conflict with a contrary insistence on white superiority (this grows more pronounced as he moves from the early novels to the later 'Zulu' novels), and no satisfactory resolution of the resulting tension is ever achieved (Street, p. 7-8).

Although Evolutionary Anthropology insisted that the savage was a remote, childlike ancestor to Western man, and hence, rather different from him; the act of placing the savage on the evolutionary tree whose most prominent upper branch was the Englishman made a study of his social customs, however foolish they might seem, a worthy enterprise. This view reinforced the conventional Western European hierarchy of human 'races' while nevertheless providing a reason for Westerners to study alien customs. This issue is treated at greater length in Chapter 3 of this book.

However, an even more 'relativistic' view of the primitive than this makes its appearance in the late nineteenth century, also. The revelation that foreign ways of life are shaped primarily by structures of social rules, an intellectual position which some attained, cleared a space for the levelling inference that 'savages' are but human beings living according to a different set of rules from those observed by the 'civilized'. One could argue that it is this intellectual position – the tendency to see social existence in terms of behaviour patterned by social codes whether written or unwritten, a 'proto-semiotic' understanding of foreign cultures – which offers the most radical challenge to the biological and 'racial' determinist theories traditionally underpinning notions of white Anglo-Saxon superiority.

While the science of Anthropology had to await the work of Malinowski and Boas in the twentieth century before it passed anything like a watershed of cultural relativism, the work of Kipling and, to a certain extent, Burton, in the nineteenth century demonstrates the existence of what might be called, at some risk of anachronism, a tradition of 'semiotic imperialism' seeking expression in the literature growing out of the imperial enterprise – an intellectual impulse in conflict with a more visible racial determinism, or, in Kipling's case, a belief that the civilizing mission of the British empire is analogous to that of the Roman. The contradictions which structure Burton's views of Eastern cultures in the 1850s, for instance, testify to an advanced but still incomplete emergence from racial determinism: his view of human social life as structured like a game or games, with rules particular to each culture, hardly rests easily on the same pages with his other, stridently ethnocentric, claims.[12] In *A Pilgrimage to El-Medinah and Mecca* (1856), for instance, an egregious racism and ethnocentrism coexist uneasily with a notable respect for, if not overvaluation of, a number of Arab customs and traditions, traditions which he claims to have observed from the inside by virtue of his clever use of disguise to penetrate the Grand Mosque in Mecca.[13] One might say that Burton's task of disguising himself imposes on him the intellectual burden of reducing Arab behaviour to rules which he must learn in order to pass as a Muslim and which he subsequently comes to see as responsible for many of the important differences between Arabs (or, more generally, Muslims) and Englishmen. In this work of the 1850s, Anglo-Saxon superiority is stressed, but the foundation for it is beginning to be undermined by a kind of qualified sympathy which is one result of the practical imperative to which he finds himself subject.

However, an important qualification is in order here. Some of Burton's 'generosity', if one might call it that, towards Arabs may be traced to the same root as Haggard's respect for the 'primitive': a note of Rousseauistic nostalgia sounds in his appreciation of Bedouin culture as more 'natural' than European ('nature is founder of customs in savage countries; whereas, among the soi-disant civilized, nature has no deadlier enemy than custom', Burton, 36).[14] While this belief in the ideal of the noble savage can often be father to a kind of condescending cross-cultural sympathy (and certainly it functions that way in Haggard), Burton's account also teems with brief but sweeping generalizations about 'character' (both national and individual) that are, notwithstanding, firmly anchored in racism, bald ethnocentrism, and the spurious claims of phrenological pseudo-science. For example, at one point he turns down one 'Shayk' who offers his services to him because a quick phrenological analysis reveals the presence of 'shiftiness'. Likewise, his broadest cultural generalizations (for instance, Egyptians are blessed with some of the qualities of good soldiers – 'mechanical dexterity' and 'stubbornness' – although they still lack the 'head' of European soldiers (Burton, p. 119)) are often based on a quite familiar body of inherited European prejudice about the people of the East.

Nevertheless, as Said reminds us, the singularity of this book lies in its analysis of social codes, not merely those governing religious activity (which is conventionally held to be rule-governed activity) but those which determine the meaning of everyday events in Muslim life: what an Indian Muslim signals when he drinks a glass of water (p. 21), how the Arab doctor's symbolic function far outweighs in importance his medical function (pp. 554-7), how the Bedouin discriminates minute landscape differences imperceptible to Westerners (p. 160), how ritual not only channels pre-existent emotion but actually produces it (p. 271). These passages produce anthropological insights of striking originality, insights which rest uneasily on the same pages with his more conventional recapitulation of the savage/civilized dichotomy. Moreover, in the process of constructing a 'Muslim' identity for himself, Burton finds himself forced to shelve temporarily his belief in racial essences, a position which, were he forced to project its implications beyond the Muslim world, would threaten the idea of European superiority.

Arriving in Cairo to book passage to Medinah early in his journey, Burton rejects as impractical the suggestion that he assume a 'positive' identity and instead decides to disguise himself as a Pathan from Rangoon: a pose of pure difference. As he reveals,

After long deliberation about the choice of nations I became a Pathan. Born in India, of Afghan parents, who had settled in the country, educated at Rangoon, and sent out to wander, as men of that race frequently are from early youth, I was well guarded against the danger of detection by a fellow countryman. To support the character requires a knowledge of Persian, Hindostani, and Arabic, all of which I knew sufficiently well to pass muster; any trifling inaccuracy was charged upon my long residence at Rangoon. (Burton, pp. 51-2)

The disguise of multiple nationality affords him obviously important advantages: (1) he need not play an Arab among Arabs, who would likely see through such a disguise eventually; (2) even were he to encounter other Afghans, traces of 'foreignness' in his speech would be attributed to habits developed in his Rangoon exile or in his other wanderings. However, beyond these practical advantages, in fact, conditioning the very possibility of the success of his disguise, lies an implicitly 'semiotic' model of cultural identity: 'nationality' is a space in a network of differences; to claim a national identity is to claim a purely differential identity. To be an Afghan is not to be an Indian, a Persian, an Arab, and so forth. There is no positive Afghan essence which one might aspire to capture. Beyond merely coming to an appreciation of the fact that human social life is structured by codes, a position to which his great 'orientalist' learning and his facility in eight different Asian languages led him, Burton comes to the verge of articulating the more radical discovery that those codes are built on networks of significant differences, for if nationality and race are not essences, then they forfeit any claim to be the ultimate determinants of fundamental human differences. The success of Burton's disguise, although analysed by him here only for its narrowly practical implications, leaves him on the verge of giving birth to an important cultural insight which, nevertheless, will remain stillborn because to acknowledge it would be to deny himself the comfort that his English sense of racial and cultural superiority affords. As the ultimately fruitless pursuit of the elusive historical original in Disraeli's *Tancred* subtly undermines the logic of a racism grounded in a belief in the existence of such an original essence, so Burton's stumbling on the purely differential nature of 'national identity' through the practical imperative of providing himself with a disguise that will pass muster is a discovery which menaces the essentialist notions of racial identity in which he also – simultaneously – exults. However, while Disraeli is intent on maintaining his Romantic allegiance to the 'original', an allegiance based on an ethnocentric subordination of world history to biblical authority, Burton is much more of a cultural relativist, commenting wryly on the superiority of Bedouin culture to the 'soft' European way of life, risking at least momentarily the psychological abyss opened up by the discovery that identities are constructed of gossamer tissues of difference.

Were he a contemporary anthropologist like Lévi-Strauss, one might expect him to treat the discovery that identities inhere, not in the external world, but in the conceptual structure which one employs to make sense of that world, as a discovery which implies the need to design a new conceptual structure – or at least to cast a hard critical eye on that which one has inherited.[15] But it would be anachronistic to ask of Burton in the 1850s anything like Lévi-Strauss's self-consciousness and methodological sophistication. For all his idiosyncrasies and the interesting intellectual perspective imposed on him by the demands of playing the Muslim, Burton nevertheless seeks refuge over and over again in conventional Victorian 'wisdom' about the East at mid-century. Like Disraeli in the 1840s, Burton has too great a stake in essentialist notions of race and nationality to discard them in the face of evidence turned up by the success of his own disguise.[16]

Nevertheless, Burton's travelogue has a wide significance because its internal stresses presage a new turn in the literature of imperialism, although that new turn will not be evident, for the most part, until the twentieth century. In the novel, the notion that a clash of cultures involves primarily a confrontation of different rule systems rather than one of 'racial' or 'national' essences is taken up by Forster in *Passage to India* (1924).[17] Yet, Forster was certainly no celebrator of the British imperial order, and his novel sets out with the conscious intention of challenging the British claim that it has a right to rule India because it 'knows' India. Even the sympathetic Fleming can never truly 'know' Aziz, in part, because Aziz is himself a fold in the everchanging fabric of Indian history. Political events of which he has become the centre have changed him by the end of that novel, denying even as sympathetic an orientalist as Fleming the chance to appropriate him as a stable object of knowledge – a precondition, Forster seems to insist, to 'friendship'. Yet the cultural codes by which Aziz lives are ultimately judged no better or worse that Fleming's.

However, Kipling's *Kim* takes on important meaning in this context. As the most instructive turn-of-the century attempt to justify England's imperial mission in the face of the levelling implications in the view that cultural differences stem primarily from differences in social codes, Kim suggests an interesting comparison with Burton's work because Kipling's discursive promotion of empire is menaced by his own strikingly similar cultural relativism. Through the central conceit of 'The Great Game', Kipling attempts to reconcile his belief in the ultimate worth of the British imperial mission (if not of Anglo-Saxon racial superiority) with an egalitarianism imposed on him by his determination to see all people as players engaged in the various games of life.[18] However, the ultimate result is ideological incoherence stemming from his failure, at the end, to expel the reader's suspicion that he is treating the 'game' of empire finally as nothing but a boy's lark.

Nevertheless, the incoherence into which Kim's imperial ideology sinks is worth examining at some length here because Kipling's attack on England's ethnocentric complacency is so far-reaching and effective. Like Disraeli's *Tancred*, like Burton's *Pilgrimage*, like the best of the century's children's literature, Kipling's *Kim* challenges the facilely ethnocentric privileging of work over play. In depicting an imperial agent whose most effective work is but a species of a more inclusive play, Kipling reverses a hierarchy which supports popular British conceptions of two analogous relationships: the superiority of the adult to the child and of the knowledgeable imperialist to the untutored, 'childlike', colonial native. Interestingly, Lewis Carroll had already, thirty-five years before *Kim* was written, drawn more strikingly radical anti-imperialist implications out of the determination to view human behaviour as a code-governed form of life in his classic 'children's' book *Alice's adventures in Wonderland.* Reversing the historical order in my examination, I will attempt here first a brief look at Kipling's – ultimately futile – effort to 'save' imperial values from the challenge his 'proto-semiotic' view of human culture poses, before moving on to an exploration of Carroll's earlier, more critical, lampoon of the logic governing cultural imperialism.

III

The two major imperial themes I have just cited – the ultimate 'motivelessness' of imperial desire and the 'proto-semiotic' view of alien cultures as code-governed forms of life – dovetail neatly in Kipling's masterwork *Kim*.[19] Through his use of the central conceit of the 'game', Kipling demonstrates both his distance from the Evangelical demand for a 'serious', 'moral' justification for empire and his determination nonetheless to find a new sanction for England's role as India's caretaker in the imperative to play the imperial game to win. Kipling endows Kim's adventures with a purpose – they are successful 'moves' in the 'Great Game' – while suggesting that, nevertheless, the 'Great Game' is still but a game.

It is impossible to miss the extent to which Kipling very carefully depicts Kim's actions as moves in various games.[20] The boy's 'privileged' position in Lahore life early in the book clearly stems, not from the fact that he is known as a sahib, but from his own demystified view of aspects of Indian life that remain clouded with a religious aura for other Indians, and this ability springs directly from the perspective afforded by his anomalous cultural status: the English boy who lives as a lower-caste Indian and speaks and thinks in a number of dialects and languages (Urdu, Punjabi, and English principal among them). Like Burton, Kim has had to learn cultural and linguistic rules as rules, for he had no 'mother's breast' from which to imbibe them. The advantage this procures for him is obvious throughout his wanderings over India: he need not fear divine punishment for breaking what are, after all, but the laws of humankind. For instance, he is rewarded with food in the bazaar because he is the only one willing to kick the Brahminee bull away from the stalls (Kim, p. 14). Moreover, his 'disenchanted' view of caste laws allows him to violate them with breezy impunity, either to disguise himself or to help others. Because of his 'unclouded' perspective and his juvenile flexibility and openness to new experience, he proves himself the perfect subject for Colonel Creighton to enlist in the English cause in 'The Great Game'.

Kim's actions eventually find their ultimate sanction as moves in this 'Game'. Because the Kiplingesque notion of 'game' is informed by a 'public school' ethos – games are contests to sort out winners from losers – games are also power contests in Kim; in other words, the rules of the game define the parameters within which a contest for superiority takes place.[21] Once Kim enlists in the 'Great Game', he is no longer engaging in pure, objectless play; his playful activity is cathected with an object: the goal of extending and reinforcing England's hold on India. 'The Great Game' becomes the *langue* which guarantees the meaning of each individual *parole* – each 'move' within it, each action which furthers the English cause.

However, Kipling complicates Kim's initiation immensely by

depicting other 'games' which also contend for his allegiance. The
Lama's search for the 'River', for example, is the principal rival to
Mahbub Ali's 'Great Game', and, at moments in the text, Kim's
primary allegiances swing to that 'Holy Man' and to the task of helping
him to free himself from the Wheel of Desire. Indeed, the renunciatory alternative represented by the Lama poses the gravest threat to
Colonel Creighton's Bildung programme for Kim, for, by threatening
desire itself, it necessarily presents a challenge to the imperial desire
into which Kim is being initiated.Thus, the Lama's search for the
'River' is initially distinguished from Kim's search for the 'Red Bull'.
In fact, early in the book the soothsayer insists that the two goals are
antithetical: the meaning of Kim's star is war while the meaning of
the Lama's is peace and the river (Kim, p.39). Yet the two searches
coincide in an uncanny way that works, or seems to work, to the
ultimate benefit of both.[22] Kim's discovery of his 'Red Bull' – his
father's regimental flag – leads him into the hands of the English army
and from there into school where, ironically, through the Lama's
financial help, he learns those skills necessary to become a full-fledged
imperial secret agent. Likewise, his travels with the Lama in search of
his 'River' afford him the chance to render surreptitious services to
other imperial agents: he transmits messages for Mahbub Ali, helps
save an English agent he meets on a train by disguising him as a
saddhu, and, most importantly, works with Huree Babu in the
Himalayas to foil the plans of the Russian spies. The clear implication
is a familiar Kiplingesque one: order, even that small degree of social
order necessary to allow the exercise of a religious life of renunciation,
can only be guaranteed by the forceful vigilance of a power – in this
case, England – strong enough to repel threats from without.[23] The
game of empire is the fundamental game because order is the
prerequisite for the playing of all games.

   However, despite the apparent claims of the 'Great Game' to be the
ultimate sanction of all actions here, the Lama's 'Middle Way' does
offer itself as a compelling rival to the 'Great Game': a game unto itself,
with its own rules and its own prescriptions for reading the meaning
of events ('moves' within the game), the Lama's 'game' has a legitimate claim to be considered at least one alternative interpretive system
worthy of respect. For instance, his Buddhist renunciatory 'Way' can
be said – in Hegelian terms – to 'comprehend' the meaning of the
Hindu doctrine of reincarnation on the Wheel: his search is admittedly
an attempt to get off the Wheel, to achieve a kind of Nirvana by putting

the cycle of reincarnation to an end – for himself, anyway ('I go to cut myself free', Kim, p. 10). In the Lama's view, the goal of life ought to be to free oneself from the endlessly repetitive cycle of reincarnation, in fact, to attain a state in which the slavish pursuit of any goal becomes irrelevant. Yet reincarnation is also (interestingly, and for an important novelistic purpose) Kipling's favourite metaphor for the metamorphoses which Kim undergoes in his development. Kim's repeated changes – the different roles he plays, the different disguises he assumes – are explicitly recovered by the Lama as 'reincarnations'. Hence, when he discovers in the army camp that Kim is a sahib, he questions him about the paradoxical fact that an erstwhile sahib should be so knowledgeable about Indian ways:

'But no white man knows the land and the customs of the land as thou knowest. How comes it this is true?'

'God knows, Holy One: but remember it is only for a night or two. Remember, I can change swiftly. It will all be as it was when I first spoke to thee under Zam-Zammeh, the great gun...'

'As a boy in the dress of white men – when I first went to the Wonder House. And a second time thou wast a Hindu. What shall thy third incarnation be?' (Kim, p. 88)

Kipling's clear implication is that playing a role in a game can be seen, in Hindu/Buddhist terms, as a reincarnation, and hence, as a capitulation to the appeal of desire, an action that *ipso facto* condemns Kim to the Wheel. Kim, much more thoroughly and in much more sophisticated fashion than Tancred, depicts a contest pitting alternative interpretive systems against each other, all of them claiming the mutually exclusive authority to 'explain' events in the narrative (and, by extension, in history).

Yet, as Kipling dangles this 'Buddhist' interpretive possibility in front of his reader's nose, he is simultaneously undermining the Lama's interpretive authority by depicting him as the most childish figure in the book. In his naïveté and rigid adherence to one role, the role of disciple of the 'Way', he functions as an ironically 'childish' counterpart to Kim's preternatural sophistication. On this view, the Lama is the most manipulated figure in the book, oblivious to the fact that his return to the Himalayas is part of a carefully contrived plan by Huree Babu to thwart the Russians' spy work, and to the fact that his own suffering under the Russian's and Frenchman's insults helps to promote the Secret Service's goal of expelling England's imperial rivals from the Himalayas. On the other hand, what Kim grows to understand in his greater wisdom is that conscious metamorphosis – the deliberate assumption of different roles, the self-conscious playing of different games – is the meaning of adulthood. 'Adulthood', in this new sense, is but a name for a more comprehensive 'childhood'. The more one plays, the more heterogeneous one's roles, the more one comes to rejoice in the play of substitution, the wiser one is. In this respect, the 'Great Game' can be said to 'comprehend' the Lama's game of renunciation of the 'illusory' world of desire: Kim ultimately celebrates the chameleon-like mutability of the imperial agents who know the rules of many games and are capable of donning many disguises. Thus, Kim rhapsodizes on the Grand Trunk after having surmounted a small rise that allows him to view all India (metaphorically anyway) in the diversity of its castes and geography: 'This is a good land – the land of the South!' (*Kim*, p. 61). By contrast, the Lama's surly response ('And they are all bound upon the Wheel. . . Bound from life after life. To none of these has the Way been shown.') reveals the self-inflicted blindness of his single-mindedness. To the Lama, the vitality and diversity of Indian life is something to be deplored. Like a Buddhist Bunyan, he deplores diversity itself as a deceptive snare: the Grand Trunk is Vanity Fair, the deceptive world of mere appearance, mere desire.

Kipling, then, inverts the traditional hierarchy of work over play – 'playing' is precisely what the most sophisticated 'adults' in this novel do best – in order to initiate Kim into an adulthood which is notable, paradoxically, for its juvenility. To delight in disguise is to delight in the power of a sense of mastery that accompanies knowledge won through a play of masks. When C. S. Lewis identified Kipling as England's foremost poet of work,[24] his critical authority retarded the overdue critical appreciation of him as a prime spokesman for play; in fact, as a novelist who sets out to undermine the facilely ethnocentric privileging of work over play or the 'serious' over the 'non-serious'. A logic which credits the nineteenth-century European distinction between work and play confronts the limits of its own usefulness to explain Kim – the boy whose play is work that retains its playfulness. Hence, when he hints early in the book to the old soldier that war is about to break out, Kipling reveals that Kim's motives are of the highest precisely because he has learned to eschew an ulterior, utilitarian, motive:

Kim warmed to the game, for it reminded him of experiences in the letter-carrying line, when, for the sake of a few pice, he pretended to know more than he knew. But now he was playing for better things – the sheer excitement and the sense of power. (Kim, p. 45)

Like Stalky, Kim indulges a youthful exuberance which is also a will-to-power potentially serviceable to English imperial objectives. Like his mentor Colonel Creighton (Kim's version of Stalky's 'Head') who wished to be a Fellow of the Royal Society ('men are as chancy as children in their choice of playthings', Kim, p. 172), work for him is a species of play. In fact, Kipling is possessed by the paradoxical question, broached by Disraeli in Tancred, of how 'youthful exuberance' can be simultaneously will-to-power (to place it in a psychoanalytic context: how 'motiveless' play can be said to have a 'motive' – mastery). In the process of examining this, Kipling looses a corrosive critique of any number of systems of authority – religious, philosophical, and political – a critique which he then attempts to arrest by the only partly successful imposition (in bad faith) of a Dantesque vision of harmonious order – the multilayered texture of concentric rule systems of which the 'Great Game"'is the greatest and most comprehensive. Kim's acceptance of any number of 'fathers' in this Bildungsroman is the prime example of his sophistication, his 'adult' ability to accept the play of substitution, but Kipling's depiction of the various conflicting religious systems of authority reveals his inability and unwillingness to locate, in any one of them, a source of universal metaphysical (or moral) authority, while conceding that, nevertheless, each has its own attenuated, provisional authority (which finally amounts to the implicit assertion that each has existence and the ability to attempt to explain events without threat of serious refutation only because each is a perfectly self-enclosed, self-justifying system). The seeds of Kipling's 'bad faith' lie precisely in this: each language (one might, without distortion, substitute 'game' here) implies its own metaphysics (as Mahbub Ali implies), but all metaphysical systems are ultimately self-enclosed and mutually exclusive – ultimately, none have universal validity, but only a provisional validity for those inside them who are willing to follow their rules. Despite this, Kipling wants to insist, the 'Great Game' is the foundation of all other games: a universal arche -game which all play although all are not conscious of their roles within it.

The main religious systems depicted here are Christianity (of a rather austere variety), Buddhism, Hinduism, and Islam. All are variously praised for their usefulness within their limited spheres while their narrowness is exposed to light. Indeed, much more successfully than Disraeli in *Tancred*, Kipling actually manages to syncretically merge various creeds in a convincing fashion that allows him to examine simultaneously their faults as well as their virtues.

For instance, as we have already hinted, the Lama's 'Way' is symbolically merged here with the 'straight and narrow' of Bunyanesque Christianity, and both are shown to share similar faults, similar deficiencies. Not only does Kipling have the Lama condemn the Vanity Fair of the Grand Trunk Road in terms that would be applauded by the most austere English Dissenter, but the narrator's celebration of Kim's openness to experience and his epic celebration of the diversity of India – 'India was awake and Kim was in the middle of it, more awake and more excited than anyone' (*Kim*, p. 71) – is an implicit repudiation of a point of view that would condemn such a pageant as but an insubstantial spectacle, a tissue of dream-like illusions. The point is that Kim and India are *awake*, and that he is in the *middle* of Indian life, as far as it is possible to get from the Lama's ascetic disdain for the ostensibly 'illusory' world of human desire. And such a disdain, Kipling is implicitly arguing, is shared by both the more severe forms of Christianity (with which Kipling was first made acquainted in the 'House of Desolation'of his childhood exile in England) and the Lama's renunciatory brand of Buddhism. In effect, Kipling is able to focus his critique of the Evangelical 'missionary' mentality by displacing it onto the Lama.

Yet, through Mahbub Ali, Kipling also acknowledges a limited respect for religious faiths, for a knowledge of such faiths has a very practical meaning for him who would traverse cultures and languages in order to manipulate believers. As he tells Kim, 'faiths are like the horses. Each has merit in its own country' (*Kim*, p. 140). In Kipling's terms, this reduces to the idea, emphasized throughout the book, that each language implies its own peculiar metaphysics: a notion very useful to the English ruling class. Thus, Father Victor, initially sympathetic to Kim's plight when they first meet at the regimental encampment, tolerates Kim's talk of miracles, not only because he is a Roman Catholic, but because he realizes that one can never gain a metaphysical understanding of another without being able to speak his language. Thus later, during his testing at the hands of Lurgan Sahib, Kim becomes the first of Lurgan's pupils to 'save' himself from shark-infested metaphysical water by forcing himself to think in

English rather than in Hindi (Kim, p. 150), a patently 'adult' act of conscious substitution which proclaims that this 'child' will never be prey to manipulation by systems of religious belief because he can consciously control the degree of his immersion in any metaphysical (linguistic and cultural) structure.

The novel then enacts Kipling's own delight in the play of substitution: play-acting, reincarnation, rebirth, renewal – these are all forms of a centrally 'motiveless' play. Systems of belief, systems of political order and hierarchy, all are subject to this play of substitution (hence, Kipling's much noted concern with the inevitable decay of all imperial achievements), a substitution which corrodes their claims to universal authority while nevertheless making the search for an authority which is not subject to this play of substitution the goal of the life Kim leads for us all. Thus, the inherently contradictory nature of Kim's plot-life is ironically summed up in the Lama's illusory metaphorical goal – the 'River', like Huck Finn's Mississippi, is the figure of metamorphosis itself, Heraclitean flux, identity in name only. To seek a river is to seek something which changes with every passing second. Thus, the contradictory nature of Kim's search for an ultimate imperial authority, a father who is privy to all the secrets of history, bears an uncanny resemblance to the Lama's pursuit of the 'goal' of 'goallessness'.

Kipling's point seems to be that metaphysical illusion is emotionally compelling. When the Lama finally 'finds' his river and attempts to baptize himself in it, to lose himself in an experience of oneness for which he has searched so long, he is, ironically, 'reborn'. Moreover, he is reborn through the mediation of Huree Babu, himself disguised as a hakim, who saves him from drowning. The ironies accumulate at this point because the Lama has discovered a need (to show his chela the Way) that grows out of the contemplation of the end of need (his vision of the oneness of things). Moreover, his rebirth places him back on the Wheel of Desire through the intervention of a master of the 'Great Game'. If the Lama's 'illusory' vision of the end of illusion can energize anyone, if his belief in the justness of the Wheel and the certainty of liberation from it ('Just is the Wheel! Certain is our deliverance.' Kim, p. 284) can compel our attention and sympathy, it can do so only because of the mediation of the imperial agent, working alone at his thankless task, in disguise, to 'save' him who would 'save' us all. A superstructure of religious and poetic 'truth' is erected on a foundation of political stability guaranteed by an empire that is only as stable and enduring as its own human agents.

Ultimately, to call such a foundation a 'game', as Kipling does, even if a 'Great Game', is to proclaim its provisional status in the same act of celebrating it as foundational. Despite his attempt to centralize it, Kipling cannot finally expel the traces of 'trivial child's play' that inhabit the Victorian meaning of 'game'. In this, Kipling pushes his logic up against the limits of his language's explanatory power, limits set by cultural constraints operating (still) on industrialized societies and which determine 'play' as what 'work' and 'moral seriousness' are not. He cannot arrest a play of substitution which is already corroding the authority of all the interpretive systems he introduces, including that of the 'Great Game' of imperial management. Ultimately, it matters little whether one calls these systems 'political' or 'religious' or 'metaphysical'. The determination to save the imperial venture from the implicit threat posed by his concomitant view of life as a series of games, this persistent 'juvenility' of outlook, leaves us as readers in the same uneasy position as Kim at the end: forced to celebrate in the language appropriate to epic the schoolboyish foiling of some rather inept spies' plans.

IV

If Kim reveals a complicity between a discourse on play and an imperial ideology whose objectives are presumably served by attracting young readers to the notion of empire as a privileged field of play, it also, as I have demonstrated, introduces an element which threatens to subvert the value of the 'work' of empire by demonstrating that the 'play of substitution' is a threat to any hierarchy or authority – religious, cultural, or political. Not surprisingly, it has often been noted that the best 'children's' literature of the nineteenth century seems to perform an analogous dual function: seeming to reinforce 'adult' values by transmitting them in a form which is palatable to children but which simultaneously introduces subversive elements to corrode the claims to authority of those values. Obviously, one cannot parody didactic poetry (as Lear and Carroll, among many others, often do) without raising questions about the worth of the sentiments voiced by the original. However, the example of Kim raises more important questions than this about the political 'innocence' of children's literature as well, largely because Kipling treats the question of political innocence as a non-issue. Naturally, children's literature has to do with politics, Kim proclaims. What, in life, does not? Moreover, to reverse or problematize the work/play hierarchy, as Kipling does, is to make a pointedly 'political' statement, regardless of how carefully one attempts to insulate oneself from the 'issues of the day'.

As the author of a work which offers a profound challenge to English ethnocentric complacency, Lewis Carroll deserves to have the political implications of his writing examined more thoroughly than they have been so far. While no one would dispute the claim that Carroll was fascinated by games and puzzles and that the Alice books constitute a frontal assault on the Victorian 'gospel of work', one might question the reason for attempting to situate him in relation to imperialism. Indeed, the evidence from his letters suggests that the man's political opinions can only be characterized as 'conventional Tory', if such a characterization did not threaten to attribute a more systematic set of political beliefs to him than either his life or letters reveal. However, it is worth noting that although he seems to have rarely turned his attention to politics, on at least one occasion when he did – at the time of the Parliamentary debate over the Second Irish Home Rule Bill – he took a characteristic delight in reducing this heated political debate to a puzzle. In fact, his 'Home Rule Mystery' was just one of many Home Rule puzzles and games introduced to the English market in the months following Gladstone's introduction of the Bill in February 1893.[25]

A man who could construct a parlour game out of an emotional political issue must, one imagines, have had an extraordinarily detached outlook on politics. Yet one need not be overly surprised that Carroll could find the imaginative material for a game in the debate over Ireland's place in the Empire. Indeed, a close look at Alice's adventures in Wonderland reveals a fascination on his part with the imaginative possibilities latent in a 'confrontation of cultures' – the kind of encounter that Kipling, with his far greater familiarity with actual cultural differences, would later explore in Kim. Perhaps Carroll was attracted by the imaginative possibilities latent in the same kind of dilemma which fired the imagination of Swift, a writer with anything but a purely playful interest in political issues: what happens when one deposits a representative of English culture in a foreign land populated by beings who live by unfamiliar rules? In short, it is time to examine Alice's relationship to imperialism, because the dilemma in which she finds herself seems designed to raise questions about her 'imperial' assumption that all discourses are either self-evidently commensurable or can be made to seem so.[26] In *Alice*, Carroll renders a world organized by game-like social structures in which mastery of the game promises mastery of others, but a world in which Alice, failing to attain such mastery, must instead resort to naked force to get her way.[27] Where Kipling employs the metaphor of the 'game' to attack English ethnocentric complacency while nevertheless justifying England's right to perform her imperial duties, Carroll explores the way in which the very process of identifying a cultural game in order to play it becomes an act of aggression. By entrapping his heroine in an ethnocentric net from which she is powerless to free herself, Carroll marks himself as a more profound – albeit indirect – critic of the epistemological foundations of cultural imperialism than Kipling would ever become.

An 'ethnographic' approach to Alice's adventures is authorized by the fact that, when Alice enters Wonderland, she finds herself in a world that appears to be, at least potentially, rule-governed, although the rules that give meaning to the behaviour of the creatures are beyond her ken and must be discovered by inference. To put it another way: more often than not, what would be 'natural' behaviour in an English setting is inappropriate in Wonderland; the social codes that determine what is or is not 'natural' are very different in the two spheres. Moreover, as Kathleen Blake has argued, language itself is viewed as a kind of game here:

To Huizinga, to the linguist Ferdinand de Saussure, and ... to Carroll too, language itself is a gamelike system of reciprocally accepted terms and rules, arbitrary, meaningful only by social arrangement. From this point of view, a realm without games is hard to imagine. (K. Blake, p. 16)

However, rules take on an even greater importance in this text than Blake will allow because, paradoxically, they are so difficult to infer. Not only is it difficult to imagine a realm without games, but the very notion that there might be a realm of experience not governed by rules is rendered highly problematic in *Alice*. The text leaves indeterminate – so, one could say, does 'life' – the question of whether or not all spheres of social existence conform to a canon of laws of one sort or another.[28] Thus, the commonplace critical assumption that rule violation can provide a clue to unmask the semiotic structure of the Wonderland world is rendered doubtful by the very fact that no one

– and especially Alice – can honestly claim to have privileged access to the rules governing the behaviour of the 'creatures', and, lacking such access, to decide such central questions as whether or not the 'creatures' are engaged in competitive games or other non-competitive activities such as rituals. In short, this is but another way of formulating the claim that Alice's 'problem' is the 'problem' of ethnocentrism, and her response to her dilemma can only be described as 'imperialistic'.

Alice recognizes what her task must be, but only to a limited extent. We know, for instance, that she is especially concerned with correctly inferring rules from the strange behaviour she sees around her, and this concern of hers extends even to herself: her own physical stature is determined by her following written rules. One of her first orders of business after falling down the rabbit hole (uninvited, of course; her adventure begins as an intrusion into the White Rabbit's home in complete disregard of even her own English canon of politeness) is to attempt to shrink herself; yet this shrinking is enabled only by her having followed the instructions written on the label attached to a bottle of liquid – 'DRINK ME' (*Alice*, p. 31). The stakes in this game of rule inference are rather high, Alice knows – at least at this point in the narrative – because one's bodily integrity is tied to one's ability to successfully follow rules:

for she had read several little stories about children who had got burnt, and eaten up by wild beasts, and other unpleasant things, all because they would not remember the simple rules their friends had taught them. (*Alice*, p. 31)

As I will demonstrate, Alice's assumption that bodily shape is somehow connected to following rules is not as odd as it might sound, given the preoccupation of *Alice's adventures in Wonderland* with the ways in which systems of rules construct behavioural norms for what is 'natural'. Bodies are not recognized here until they are named – that is, classified – but even then, misrecognition is an everpresent pitfall because of the lack of a universal code. Bodies are as closely linked to the semiotic structure of the Wonderland social system as are the 'events' in which Alice participates. Alice's use of the term 'creatures' – both an insulting term which diminishes the Wonderland beings and a class name which keeps open their indeterminate status in the scale of creation (are they animal or human?) – renders their fuzzily indeterminate status: they are, perhaps, merely animate or 'animated'.

In the case of Wonderland social 'events', the resemblance between their Wonderland names and the names of similar events in nineteenth-century England misleads Alice into mistakenly assimilating them to those familiar to her. For instance, the 'caucus-race' in which Alice finds herself involved bears few of the features an English public schoolboy would associate with racing: the shape of the race-course seems arbitrarily designed; the contestants do not line up together; and the 'race' has no clearly defined beginning or ending in time (*Alice*, p. 48). The fact that the event ends with all contestants having been declared winners and all handed prizes suggests that it is not a contest at all, an inference justified by its name: the word 'caucus', at the time a relatively recent linguistic import into Victorian England from the United States, carries the implication of a meeting to iron out differences in order to present a united front for exerting political pressure – a local game of political accommodation within a larger adversarial context – rather than a contest with winners and losers.[29] If there are to be 'losers', they exist outside of the caucus, not within it. Actually, the entire 'race' aspect of the 'caucus-race' is eventually de-emphasized here in favour of the ceremony of awarding prizes, a ritual which even Alice is forced, quite against her initial impulse, to observe with a show of outward solemnity (*Alice*, p. 50).

The event is significant because it raises the same crucial question about Alice's problems of interpretation throughout her Wonderland adventure to which I have already alluded. Rituals, like games, are rule-governed social events; however, unlike games, rituals are seldom held for the purpose of sorting out winners from losers. Obviously the whole notion of 'winning' is irrelevant to most ritual events. But Alice fails miserably at this central hermeneutic task of sorting out rituals from games in Wonderland, because the names of the events misleadingly obscure the distinction between the 'large events' here and the events bearing similar names in English life.

Alice's inability to make these distinctions is the kind of myopia that will eventually result in her complete disruption of Wonderland society in a fit of almost 'missionary' zealotry at the end of the book. Thus, not surprisingly, her entrance into the garden and onto the Queen's Croquet-Ground – another of her many intrusions – is preceded by a vow that takes on a rather sinister resonance when seen in this light: 'I'll manage this time' (*Alice*, p. 104). What she 'manages' is to assimilate the game of Wonderland 'croquet' to her own English version of croquet, judge the Wonderland version to be an impossible version of the English one, and completely misinterpret the significance of the Queen's infamous command ('Off with his head!') as an event that intrudes on the game from beyond its structure of rules, despite the compelling evidence that it may well be an event within the 'game' rather than *outside* it.

Although Wonderland 'croquet' does bear some superficial resemblance to the English game (taking out the garbage bears a superficial resemblance to checkers, as well, if one views the event from a certain angle and allows for differences of scale), Alice is convinced that she can compete successfully – although she becomes frustrated with the difficulty. Characteristically, her exasperation soon boils over into the childish assumption, not that it is a difficult game, but that it is a game without rules. As she tells the Cheshire Cat,

'I don't think they play at all fairly . . . and they all quarrel so dreadfully one can't hear oneself speak – and they don't seem to have any rules in particular: at least, if there are, nobody attends to them – and you've no idea how confusing it is all the things being alive...' (*Alice*, p. 113)

Alice has no vantage-point from which to judge whether the creatures are following or breaking the rules. In circular fashion, she infers that there are rules from the fact that she has just been struggling to play by them correctly; moreover, her assumption that this Wonderland 'game' of 'croquet' is identifiable with the English version is a doubtful one, given the fact that the Wonderland event is one which one of the players – the Queen – cannot 'lose'. Her leap to the conclusion that there are 'no rules' governing this event on the Queen's croquet-ground is merely one of many instances in the text wherein her exasperation with her own ignorance or lack of skill is projected onto the 'creatures'. Alice has an imperial penchant for producing her own self-justifying evidence, as well as an exasperating (although, perhaps, understandably human) tendency to rationalize her own failures of comprehension.

Thus, Alice's judgement that the Queen's execution orders make her 'savage' (Mad Tea-Party), comes from her too-comfortable application of the rules of English croquet to the Wonderland game. Although she notes that no one ever seems actually to get beheaded (*Alice*, p. 112), she is incapable of processing the implications of that observation. The 'order' – 'Off with his head!' – does not seem to be a performative in the Wonderland linguistic universe (nor does the Duchess's 'Chop off her head!' in the 'Pig and Pepper' chapter); but because Alice has only her own English framework on which to fall back, she assumes that it must carry performative force. A more reasonable inference would be that the Queen's 'savage' order is actually a part of the game rather than an event that intrudes from outside the game. After all, Alice does notice that the King pardons all those the Queen has condemned. She might have more reasonably inferred from that fact that the event called 'croquet' in Wonderland is actually a ritual intended to reinforce the power of the King and Queen over life and death, possibly by enacting a pageant of condemnation followed by forgiveness. Not only does this inference help explain the strange fact that no one in Wonderland is ever beheaded, but, by identifying the event as a ritual, one accounts for the odd fact that this 'game' is a game which one player cannot lose. However, such an inference would require of Alice the flexibility to assign different boundaries to the 'game' of Wonderland croquet.

My intent in offering this interpretation is not to insist on a unitary decoding of the behaviour of the 'creatures', nor, tiresomely, to take Alice to task for childish naïveté. Other equally reasonable explanations might be adduced to account for the same evidence. My point is only that Alice's assuming that Wonderland 'croquet' is a competitive game says more about her own ethnocentrism than it accounts for the behaviour of the 'creatures'. Carroll has constructed a world that is radically indeterminate, a world which resists her attempt to frame the meaning of events. One needs to know the *langue* as well as the *parole*, the system as well as the individual gesture which has meaning only within that system, to make valid inferences about the meaning of events and behaviour. Alice's 'imperialism', such as it is, is a semiotic imperialism: she is incapable of constructing, on a model radically different from her own, the 'system' or 'systems' which give meaning to the behaviour of the creatures.[30]

Alice's encounter with the hookah-smoking caterpillar underlines the kind of invasive intruder she has become in Wonderland. The hookah, itself a stock 'orientalizing' feature, highlights the caterpillar's foreignness, but the tautological turn that their conversation takes demonstrates, not that the caterpillar is incorrigibly illogical, but that he refuses to be comprehended by Alice's categories of meaning. In this instance, Alice attempts to read the caterpillar's feelings by analogy with her own in order to impose her own on him (a gesture simultaneously naïve *and* imperious). He *should* feel that physical metamorphosis is 'very confusing' because she *has*. Of course, where metamorphosis is the norm, the illusion of stasis must 'feel very queer', so another sign of Alice's naïveté is the fact that she has it all wrong here. When the caterpillar resists her attempt to comprehend his experience – 'Not a bit' (Alice, p. 68) – she immediately resorts to her favourite form of aggression – making herself look larger:

'Well, perhaps your feelings may be different', said Alice: 'all I know is, it would feel very queer to me.'
    'You!' said the Caterpillar contemptuously. "Who are you ?'
    Which brought them back again to the beginning of the conversation.
Alice felt a little irritated at the Caterpillar's making such very short remarks, and she drew herself up and said very gravely, 'I think you ought to tell me who you are, first.' (Alice, p. 68)

In the Hegelian game of 'comprehension' that is being played out here, Alice's frustration with her inability to comprehend the experience of the caterpillar (he who closes the circle of the tautology defeats the other's attempt to know him) causes her to resort to literalizing what she is talking about: she tries to makes herself appear larger than he. The pun on 'short' shifts the discourse back to a literal surface, and she attempts to grow to meet the caterpillar's challenge – the challenge of incomprehensibility – by bullying. But the disjunction in the text between 'comprehending' and 'growing larger than' (Alice knows least when she is the largest, as in the White Rabbit's house where she cannot perceive what is going on outside, or at the end of the trial where she surrenders all hope of understanding the event in favour of pure disruption) is reinforced in this passage, and suggests that Carroll is lampooning the Hegelian equation of 'comprehension' with knowledge – precisely the equation which Sandison notes underlies the epistemological form of nineteenth-century imperialism (Sandison, p. 60). 'Growing' becomes a poor substitute for 'knowing' here and its insufficiency inevitably draws Alice into a game of violent disruption. Growing is both Alice's substitute for the object of knowledge which she cannot successfully appropriate and a sign of her incomprehension – thus, the disjunction.

To Hegel, of course, the route to knowledge is via appropriation: the highest form of consciousness is self-consciousness, but self-consciousness that is recognized by an other.[31] As the philosopher, writing the Phenomenology of mind in his study within hearing range of Napoleon's guns at the Battle of Jena, 'comprehends' the world-historical figure of Napoleon by constructing a history that includes him in a teleological process culminating in Hegel's own moment of writing, so Alice must grow to 'comprehend' that which she would know; although, as already mentioned, the few times she does experience 'growth' in Wonderland take her away from self-consciousness – knowledge – rather than toward it.[32] Alice's struggle for recognition by the creatures – her will-to-master – drives her beyond any bounds of decency (if it were possible to conceptualize a set of 'decency rules' not bound by constraints of time, place, and culture). If there is rule violation in this text, surely Alice is the violator *par excellence.*

The relevance of Hegel's notion of the desire for 'recognition' as the driving force behind Alice's will to manage the 'creatures' casts some light on some of the more puzzling problems of identity which she confronts. Alice perfectly embodies the Hegelian paradox of identity, the 'doubling' that is at the basis of his notion of subjectivity. The imperative that drives the Hegelian 'master' to risk his life for recognition involves him in a kind of enslavement to the other: he seeks to attain pure 'self-consciousness', but 'self-consciousness' that is 'recognized' by the other – the 'slave' – who is himself unselfconscious and fears to put himself at risk.[33] Thus, Alice's initial splitting of self in the 'Pool of Tears' episode (she becomes both addresser and addressee of her own discourse, performer of feats and self-applauder, the measurer and the measured) provides her with her own 'slaves' to accord her recognition and presages the way in which she will attempt to treat the 'other' when she confronts him directly: as putty to be shaped in accordance with her own wishes. Not surprisingly, when she meets the mouse after having fallen into her own pool of tears, she immediately gives offence: 'Où est ma chatte?' (*Alice*, p. 42). And in no time, she is adding insult to injury by attempting to forcibly embrace him in an false community with herself signalled by her use of the word 'we'. The 'otherness' of the other is barely acknowledged by Alice in this book, yet paradoxically, recognition by the other is precisely what she most avidly seeks. All discourse is a species of oneiric discourse here, as the Hegelian 'master's' drive for recognition is marked by a condition impossible to satisfy: to be recognized by the other is implicitly to reduce the other forcibly to the condition of recognizing without herself being recognized in turn; however, the price one pays for being recognized as master is the knowledge that the recognizer is not himself a 'master', ultimately, not one whose recognition is worth acquiring.

Alice's frustration with the contradictions inherent in her Hegelian drive to attain mastery is evident virtually everywhere. She desires recognition but is frustrated with those who ought to be according it to her – the mere 'creatures' who have the effrontery to resist her; the beings whose 'illogical' games she is incapable of mastering. Her complaints about how the 'creatures' argue, such as in her confrontation with the Frog-Footman in the 'Pig and Pepper' chapter, display her propensity to return this frustration by projecting it outward:

'How am I to get in?' asked Alice again, in a louder tone.
  'Are you to get in at all?' said the Footman. 'That's the first question, you know.'
  It was, no doubt: only Alice did not like to be told so. 'It's really dreadful,' she muttered to herself, 'the way all the creatures argue. It's enough to drive one crazy!' (*Alice*, p. 81)

Thus, she slides immediately from the dim recognition that she perhaps has no right of entry into the Duchess's house to the abrasive assumption that the 'creatures' are overly argumentative because they too frequently frustrate her will. Her 'will-to-mastery' has both these contradictory 'subjective' and 'objective' facets: she is incapable of understanding the 'creatures' because of her own ethnocentrism and frustrated in her attempts to get them to recognize her by dominating them. In some fundamental respects, the 'creatures' refuse to engage her at all: neither acknowledging her right to 'read' them in her own ethnocentric way nor surrendering their right to 'read' her as they please. At times in this book, such as in her confrontation with the caterpillar, their outright refusal to be 'read' goads her into the bullying gestures that are the last resort of one driven to be recognized by those to whom she refuses recognition.

  Alice's difficulty with understanding the references of names in this book casts light on the disjunction between her own linguistic categories and those of the 'creatures'. She gains a taste of what it is like to be mistakenly classified when the pigeon calls her, in one of her long-necked moments, a 'serpent'. The pigeon's mistake, if one might call it that, is one to which Alice is continually prey: she abstracts certain essential properties (long-necked, egg-eating) and classifies Alice accordingly with the name she uses for all creatures who exhibit those qualities (*Alice*, p. 75). This lesson in mistake classification, however, apparently avails Alice nought, for in the Duchess's house she generates a great deal of misplaced sympathy for the 'creature' called 'Pig':

'Oh, please mind what you're doing!' cried Alice, jumping up and down in an agony of terror. 'Oh, there goes his precious nose!' as an unusually large saucepan flew close by it, and very nearly carried it off.

'If everybody minded their own business,' the Duchess said, in a hoarse growl, 'the world would go round a deal faster than it does.' (*Alice*, p. 84)

As Alice soon discovers, the 'baby' really is a pig, and thus, one would think, Alice 'ought' to have gleaned the lesson that names attempt to arbitrarily arrest the phenomenal flux by 'picking out' as essential properties those which are perhaps characteristic of merely one stage of metamorphosis (and thus, are not then truly 'essential'). Thus, the caterpillar's privileged role in this book as counterpart of Alice: what is the essence of the being we call, at merely one stage of his metamorphosis, 'caterpillar'? Carroll later parodies this form of essentialist classification in the Mock Turtle episode, where bodily essences come to be defined, in teleological fashion, as meat for the table.

When Alice next invades the 'Mad Tea-Party' to which, as the March Hare reminds her, she was not invited, her problems with naming multiply as she attempts to make sense of what seems on the surface to be a quintessentially English activity – the tea party. However, the activity in which the Mad Hatter and company are engaged can only be yoked by violence to the English conception. Once again, Alice is oblivious to the few clues to the meaning of the 'creatures" behaviour that do come her way. However, as occurs often in the history of imperialism, the intruder and natives do achieve at least a provisional sort of mutual accommodation that disguises, at least temporarily, the fact that they live by completely different social codes.[34]

For instance, Alice is initially puzzled about the fact that the table seems to be laid for a great number of guests, although only the Hatter, Hare, and Dormouse are present. Yet the Hatter offers an explanation which seems to be provisionally acceptable to both the 'creatures' and Alice:

'Well, I'd hardly finished the first verse,' said the Hatter, 'when the Queen bawled out "He's murdering the time! Off with his head!"'

'How dreadfully savage!' exclaimed Alice.

'And ever since that,' the Hatter went on in a mournful tone, 'he won't do a thing I ask! It's always six o'clock now.' A bright idea came into Alice's head. 'Is that the reason so many tea-things are put out here?' she asked.

'Yes, that's it,' said the Hatter with a sigh: 'It's always tea-time, and we've no time to wash the things between whiles.'

'Then you keep moving round, I suppose?' said Alice.

'Exactly so,' said the Hatter: 'As the things get used up.'

'But what happens when you come to the beginning again?' Alice ventured to ask.

'Suppose we change the subject,' the March Hare interrupted, yawning. 'I'm getting tired of this. I vote the young lady tells us a story.' (*Alice*, p. 99)

This passage casts interesting light on Alice's problems of interpretation for the paradoxical reason that it seems to be one of the few moments in the text when Alice can find common ground with the 'creatures'. However, when she judges the Queen's order 'savage', she does so only after having made a leap across linguistic levels of which she is oblivious. To judge the order 'savage', she must interpret the statement 'He's murdering the time!' figuratively and the statement 'Off with his head!' literally, yet she gives no hint that she is aware she has made such a leap. Had she read both literally, she would have been bound to hold the Hatter in some sort of moral abhorrence, regardless of whether she felt he was unjustly served by the Queen's order (and the Hatter's later personification of 'Time' suggests he may well be justifiably seen as a 'murderer' in at least a provisional sense – like Alice, though, the reader has no privileged access to the Hatter's system either). Lacking a framework for interpreting the 'creatures'' words in their own way, she has no metalinguistic indicators to help her decide when to take something literally or figuratively.

The one seemingly successful inferential leap Alice makes in this passage – her determination that Time's decision to stand still has frozen the Mad Hatter and March Hare into a perpetual tea-time – is actually a glaring example of the limitations imposed by her rigid conventionality: she 'naturally' assumes that tea-time is determined by the position of the hands on the clock. A more complex inference might be that in a world of perpetual tea-time, there is no other time from which tea-time may be distinguished: in effect, that there is no 'time' in the English sense, since time is an inference one ordinarily makes from changing events. Alice is the 'illogical' one here (that is, she is haunted by metaphysical ghosts), because she takes time to be the grounding of events rather than events to be the grounding of time. Thus, the Mad Hatter's response ('It's always tea-time, and we've no time to wash the things between whiles') might well refer to the lack of a servant, named 'Time', who will do the dishes for them: at least a potentially 'reasonable' response from one whose thinking is not afflicted, as Alice's is, by the reified metaphysical entity she calls 'time'.

As the archetypal imperial child, Alice must press on with her metaphysical inquiries, seemingly unconscious of their metaphysical nature. Having been told that the party moves on as the 'things get used up', she asks the question that one eventually hears from all children: 'But what happens when you come to the beginning again?' In one sense, the answer is death: the end of the chain of nourishment, the end of the process of displacement. Yet the March Hare's yawning response suggests that he has taken the question in its most boringly trivial sense: a question of the same order as the child's query about the infinite regress – 'If God made us, who made God?' It is unanswerable because it is a question about a cyclical process cast in linear terms, and a circle has no 'beginning'.

Thus, Alice finds herself posing riddles that have no answers, the very thing for which she reproached the Hatter earlier (Alice, p. 97). The cyclical nature of her adventure in Wonderland – pure metamorphosis without a telos, a process which denies her the retrospective 'knowledge' that closure brings – itself resembles the way the society of the Mad Hatter and March Hare 'appears' to her. As should be clear by now, Alice's quest to master the game of Wonderland is doomed to failure because she will never achieve the kind of self-transcendence necessary to 'comprehend' (and dominate) the 'creatures'. Her quest to learn the rules that will 'explain' their behaviour – a 'mastercode' which will provide the key to understanding their behaviour without itself presupposing the categories of their language – is doomed to frustration. She is bound to repeat the mistakes she attributes, in her pig headed way, to them. Like any good imperialist, then, Alice assumes that because she comes to play a role in the 'creatures'' drama by virtue of her undismissable presence, she can thereby dominate it, and successful domination must be the inevitable reward of 'comprehension'.[35] Of course, as has been certainly clear from at least the time of Freud, playing a role in a drama is precisely that which disqualifies one from offering a useful interpretation of the meaning of that drama, for that is the privilege of him who stands *outside* .[36] Although Alice stands outside of the 'creatures'' social system (or systems), she does not stand outside her own which she has instead elevated into a universal interpretive system called upon to explain all behaviour everywhere.

Fittingly, the Hare's request for a story (a narrative might, because it is finite and linear, provide at least a provisional closure to remove Alice and the 'creatures' from their cyclical stasis) is picked up by the Dormouse, who begins to tell a tale that is ultimately disrupted by

Alice's persistent questioning. The Dormouse's story appears to take him across linguistic boundaries in ways unacceptable to Alice: the pun on 'drawing' sends him from describing how the 'three sisters' were attempting to 'draw' treacle from a well they were 'in', to describing how they 'drew' everything with an 'M' (*Alice*, p. 102-3). Whether this story is an 'acceptable' tale or not cannot be judged without assuming the kind of universal perspective that Alice's conventionality leads her to believe she has always had. For instance, only the conclusion of the tale (which, ironically, Alice ultimately prevents him from telling) could cast retrospective light on the meaning of its elements.[37] Thus, the Dormouse casts his frustration with Alice's interruptions in the form of a sulky remark which, for all that, forecasts Alice's role as the writer of her own story in Wonderland: 'If you can't be civil, you'd better finish the story for yourself' (*Alice*, p. 101). What Carroll presents in *Alice* is a world in which those who cannot be 'civil' have no choice but to 'finish' the story for themselves, but 'finishing' here means 'enacting' it – 'playing it out' – rather than 'telling' it from a safe preserve beyond the point of closure.[38] Like the three sisters in the Dormouse's tale, Alice lives at the bottom of the well out of which she is trying to draw treacle.

In a sense, one can see Alice's 'problem' as a problem of dealing with the consequences that stem from her living in a 'decentred' world: she must re-establish 'precedence' in all its senses for herself – temporal, spatial, political, and interpretive – so that her own position as – impossibly – both master in the master/slave drama and Hegelian 'Wise Man' who lives beyond a point of closure outside of the 'game' is preserved – to re-establish herself, in effect, in the centre (which is also the end).[39] As this work makes clear, all of these senses of 'precedence' are beholden to a political relationship of domination: the foundation for this domination is always force, but, insofar as one relies on force to order the world one claims to be trying to understand, one alters and distorts what one seeks to comprehend.[40] There is an anthropological Indeterminacy Principle in operation here that underlines the untenable nature of Alice's dual Hegelian position: she cannot cast herself in the role of both 'master' and 'Wise Man' at the same time, immersed in a struggle for the control of meanings and yet calmly, disinterestedly, detached from the action as well, paring her fingernails as she simply observes a pattern of social meaning laying itself out before her. The parallel between this and Western Europe's imperial experience in the nineteenth century is close for, as

Said demonstrates, the imperial field became, during this century, a field not simply ordered by Western power but also appropriated by Western knowledge (Said, p. 12).

Thus, throughout her adventures, Alice seeks to establish temporal precedence (cf. the trial at the end where she insists on the 'proper' order of 'evidence to judgement to sentencing'), spatial precedence (e.g. at the tea table and elsewhere), political precedence (does the Queen actually have the power to execute her?), in order, ultimately, to impose her own 'interpretive' precedence – the power of the interpreter to dominate her material, the ability to 'manage' and 'make sense out of' unruly matter by extracting herself from that which she would interpret, ultimately an assertion of the primacy of the interpreter over the mere material, the right of Alice the child-imperialist to impose a meaning on the behaviour of the illogical 'creatures'.

Ultimately, all of these forms of precedence are based on the Hegelian epistemological model which privileges the geometric or 'spatial' metaphor of 'comprehension'. To 'comprehend' is to metaphorically enclose within a field some matter which is thereby made available to be 'known', or mastered.[41] Alice stands 'outside' of that which she would master only in the limited sense that she does not share the social codes of the 'creatures'. However, that position – the privilege of the alien – affords her no advantage here; in fact, it is her prime disadvantage. To play the game without knowing the rules is to be played by the game: to be inside the game while pretending to 'comprehend' it from the outside. However, to be inside the game on these terms is to be at the distinct disadvantage that he who plays without knowing the rules experiences.[42]

'The Queen's Croquet-Ground' chapter, then, is dominated by Alice's attempting to gauge the power of the 'savage' Queen, a task at which she is unsuccessful because of the ethnocentric cast of her outlook: her knowledge is perfectly circular in the sense that it consists solely in what she already knew before coming to Wonderland – in this case, the rules of the English game of 'croquet' and the official power of the King and Queen over life and death. When she visits the Mock Turtle and the Gryphon, though, she becomes involved in a wholesale questioning of the value of 'explanations' ('translations' might be a better word) over 'repetitions' that casts new light on the tautologies of the caterpillar (or rather, would cast new light on it for Alice if she were capable of processing it).

The Queen had earlier warned Alice (in an oblique way, of course, guaranteed to go right over her head) that the 'Mock Turtle' is but a creature whose purpose it is to become a meal: 'It's the thing Mock Turtle Soup is made from' (*Alice*, p. 124). Not surprisingly, when Alice meets the Mock Turtle and Gryphon, she finds them addicted to the same kinds of teleological explanation which she favours (albeit of an unfamiliar sort). In addition, the Mock Turtle seems dissatisfied (as was Alice earlier) with mere tale-telling; he purports to want 'explanation' cast in a metalanguage ('Explain all that', *Alice*, p. 138).

Thus, it is not surprising that the beings about which they discourse all seem to be creatures whose 'animal' existence is but prelude to their ultimate end as meals: they can be 'understood' as 'essentially' meals.[43] In fact, Alice even describes (unwittingly, of course) the whiting as configured in a way (tails in mouths: cf. 'tales' in mouths) that represents emblematically the circularity of all her attempts to find an explanatory metalanguage. As the Mock Turtle so aptly puts it: 'No wise fish would go anywhere without a porpoise' (*Alice*, p. 137). The mere fact that 'eating' or 'being eaten' appears to be the *telos* of most of the creatures discussed suggests that events in Wonderland have assumed a distinctively oral 'Alicean' cast – a hermeneutic circle from which Alice will never break free.[44] Carroll's obsession with 'orality' or oral forms of incorporation here is his way of working out the visible consequences of the kind of 'imperialistic recentring' in which Alice engages: to define animals teleologically as meat for the table is but a thin disguise for a process which 'recentres' Alice at the end of the chain of nourishment; for in Alice's universe, meals ultimately exist for the *purpose* of being eaten by human beings like herself.

One of the other senses of 'repetition' here must be understood in opposition to 'explanation' – reinscription in a different language. However, Alice's confessed inability to 'repeat' (everything comes out 'wrong', i.e. different) is a sign of her inability to close her own Hegelian circle and achieve 'self-consciousness'. What she asks of herself is 'repetition'; what she demands of the 'creatures' is 'explanation'. In both quests she is frustrated. In the Mock Turtle, she meets a 'creature' who throws her own demands back upon her: he 'repeats' her own imperial highhandedness. He is dissatisfied with her recitation of 'T'is the Voice of the Lobster' because he is finally only interested in 'explanation' (*Alice*, p. 139), but in reproaching Alice for not casting her account in a language outside of the language of the 'original', he insinuates that he takes a slightly different sense of 'repetition': "'What is the use of repeating all that stuff," the Mock Turtle interrupted, "if you don't explain it as you go on?'" (*Alice*, p. 140). Thus, he apparently ignores the fact that Alice, as she just 'explained', cannot 'repeat', all in order to distinguish his sense of 'explanation' from mere 'repetition' – tale-telling or poetic recitation, regardless of whether or not the teller has ever 'told' the tale before.

Thus this ambiguity inherent in the term 'repeat' (it means both 'recite' and 'repeat', but is any poetic recitation ever truly a 'repetition' of a previous recitation?) becomes a play on words here, the interplay between Alice and the Mock Turtle returns their discourse once again to the linguistic surface, and Alice misses another opportunity to read her difference from the 'creatures' out of the differing ways in which each uses words. Ironically, then, the Mock Turtle 'appears' different from Alice (and thus, difficult to understand) for the paradoxical reason that he 'appears' to be her repetition: the annoyingly obtuse visitor constantly in search of 'explanation'. In effect, the circularity of her journey in Wonderland, a circularity guaranteed by the failure of her powers of inference, places Alice in a position guaranteed to feed her already prodigious megalomania. The Mock Turtle is then aptly named for his propensity to 'mock' the alien intruder by parodying her. More generally, Alice is incapable of drawing the line between the mockery directed at her and behavioural customs that have their origin in Wonderland but which we need not see as necessarily directed at her.

What I have implicitly been arguing is that the imperial attempt to 'know' is not stymied by its inevitable failure; on the contrary, the 'failure' to know is itself converted into a 'successful' act of imperial appropriation through the imposition of a discourse which, in circular fashion, finally 'produces' the sought-for objects of knowledge. However, it is necessarily important to distinguish this form of recuperation from, say, a discovery of the ultimate commensurability of seemingly incommensurable discourses – the kind of untenable claim to universal truth which 'epistemology' makes, according to Rorty. Thus, Alice's 'failure' to 'comprehend', say, the game of Wonderland 'croquet' is appropriated as a 'success' of an imperial sort (albeit of the solipsistic variety) when she 'naturalizes' it as an English game which the 'creatures' merely play badly – both out of an 'under-standable' fear of the Queen and out of an 'incomprehensible' use of inappropriate instruments (flamingoes and hedgehogs rather than wooden mallets and balls, as any good Englishman would use).

However, as we have already seen, other ways of accounting for the same appearances are possible. The trial of the Knave of Hearts, then, extends this process even further. Because the 'creatures' really 'botch' the whole business of justice, in Alice's view, she must set them straight by teaching them the rules for conducting 'proper' trials. However, in the process of appropriating the Wonderland notion of 'trial' to her own, Alice violently reinscribes the activity she observes into her own conventional canon of precedence, and, in consequence, makes herself the centre rather than the periphery of the action: another solipsistic re-centring which ultimately makes this rather limited little girl self-appointed judge, jury, and executioner of all the 'creatures'.

That Alice's Wonderland adventure comes to a close with a 'trial' is only fitting, given the fact that the cultural ritual of the trial holds an obviously pre-eminent place in the English system of determining truth. The English 'trial' is, above all, a linearly-structured event which produces truth retrospectively by closure: when the trial is over – when the accusation has been read, the evidence presented and then weighed by the jury, and sentence pronounced by the judge – the truth is known.[45] The evidence is presented so that the jury (or judge) can place it in a retrospective order, enclose it in a field, to make it suitable for judgement. Because the truth cannot be known until all the evidence is in and weighed, the truth cannot be given an accessible form until after the point of closure. Ultimately, this is but to state the obvious: that judgement and guilt (as well as retrospection itself) are necessarily tied to a linear (narrative) model of the unfolding of events.

Not surprisingly, when the King follows the reading of the accusation with what to Alice seems a peremptory charge, 'Consider your verdict' (*Alice*, p. 146), Alice assumes the position of judge of the judge in order to impose her own notion of 'proper' temporal precedence: first, accusation, then, presentation of evidence, and finally, judgement. This role of Alice's is re-emphasized later when, in the process of giving her testimony, she lectures the King on the necessity of attaching the 'proper' label to the 'oldest rule in the book' ('it ought to be Number One', *Alice*, p. 156): another glaring instance of her own presumptuous elevation of the merely conventional to the status of universal.

Once again, however, Alice's aggressive attempt to reshape the Knave's 'trial' in a way acceptable to her guarantees that she will be unable to understand what is actually going on while ensuring that her only possible response can be an aggressive one: in this episode, a reduction of the 'creatures' to a 'mere' pack of two-dimensional cards that, nevertheless, somehow unaccountably have played her. Certainly, Alice is oblivious to the cultural significance of the event once again: what kind of 'trial' is it in which the guilty party is foreordained by a nursery rhyme cited at the beginning and in which the allegedly 'stolen' tarts are entered in evidence because of the impossible fact that they haven't been eaten? Like the Queen's 'croquet-match', this event bears the signs of a predestined ritual rather than of an open-ended 'contest' which can only be decided as it draws to a close.

Not surprisingly, it is the Hatter who is called as the first 'witness'. When he enters the courtroom carrying his everpresent teacup still filled with some 'unfinished' tea, we are reminded of the endless (and beginningless) tea party which functions both as a hint of the difference between Wonderland and nineteenth-century England and as a sign of the hermeneutic circle in which Alice is caught. In giving his 'evidence', the Hatter is asked to perform what seem to be the usual acts of retrospection Alice would 'naturally' expect of a witness. However, his testimony is a brilliant defeat of the very notion of 'testimony', and, a fortiori, retrospection: not only does he never succeed in re-presenting what the March Hare and Dormouse 'said' (*Alice*, p. 148-9), but he punctuates his account by recurring, again and again, to the banal events of his everyday life (drinking tea, buttering bread), events which are notable only for their unhistoricity, singular only in the unsingular way they repeat themselves endlessly, marking the cyclical repetitiveness of his static, undifferentiated, tea-party life. The Hatter ironically demonstrates the link between history and retrospection by subverting the latter: asked to 'remember', he can only dredge up a litany of the same.

The various threats of execution which pepper the book thus appear to be futile attempts to impose a closure on the otherwise cyclical events, a closure that would generate meaning by enabling a retrospective sorting: precisely the kind of 'closure' Alice so avidly seeks. Thus, when the King threatens execution for the Hatter's poor powers of retrospection ('You must remember, . . . or I'll have you executed', *Alice*, p. 149), he suggests, in inverted form, that execution – the closure of death – is precisely that which would enable the retrospective imposition of meaning by precipitating the Hatter out of his cyclical life of endless repetition, endless substitution of teacup for teacup. However, as we have already seen, none of the Wonder-land execution threats carry performative force. Thus, it is left to Alice to perform a final 'execution' of all the 'creatures' (by reducing them to 'only' a pack of cards), a violent closure which, ironically, merely shuffles them rather than sorts them out and assigns them a meaning. The ending precipitates Alice out of the 'creatures'' universe while denying her the power to frame her experience in a meaningful way (although she does recuperate it as the pure dross of a 'dream'), a framing power which is ostensibly the boon granted to her who steps 'outside'. Rather, the price she pays for stepping out of the 'card game' in which she was somehow played is the inability to make sense of the game.

The final chapter, then, merely leaves Alice enclosed within her own ethnocentric walls while suggesting that the Wonderland ritual of the trial follows rules quite different from any of which Alice has ever heard. The debate over the origin of the verses which are entered in evidence (are they the Knave's? they neither bear his signature nor are inscribed in his handwriting) underlines the impossible herme-neutic task faced by any representative of Western civilization who wishes to actually 'understand' what is going on here. For one thing, the question of precedence is introduced immediately by the Rabbit's question 'Where shall I begin?'(Alice, p. 158). The King's banal response – 'Begin at the beginning, ... and go on till you come to the end: then stop' – immediately calls attention to the purely conven-tional status of a manner of reading which would seem necessarily 'natural'and 'universal'. For Alice to make such a statement would be taxing the limits of our readerly patience by having her render a truism; for the King to say it, though, is to suggest both that he has assumed the Mock Turtle's role as parodic 'repetition' of Alice the 'privileged' interpreter and that, perhaps, such a statement is actually necessary because not self-evident to the 'creatures' attending at the ritual (or, possibly, that the ritual nature of the event renders all state-ments made within it purely incantatory). Given what we know of the 'circular' appearance of events in Wonderland, the King's words might well be taken as a novel prescription for properly unfolding 'evidence' (or, the King's lunacy might well be ignored by the others as a pro forma gesture of respect for his symbolic role).

When the King then proceeds to gloss the verses which he is using to condemn the Knave, he does so not because it matters to the

prosecution of the case ('If there's no meaning in it . . . that saves a
world of trouble, you know, as we needn't try to find any', *Alice*, p.
159) but because such an effort is its own reward — for obscure
reasons. In this, he recapitulates Alice's own hermeneutic effort with
similar results: the verses are pressed into service of the King's
intention of condemning the Knave by being shown to imply that the
return of the tarts to the Queen is evidence of the Knave's guilt (*Alice*,
p. 160). Once again, the cyclical nature of Alice's hermeneutic
adventure is recapitulated in the 'creatures'' own tautological enter-
prises.

The return to the frame at the end of the book provides a rather
ambiguous closure. Alice's sister substitutes herself for Alice and
recapitulates the Wonderland adventures in her own dream, although
with an important difference: in Coleridgean fashion, she only 'half
believed herself in Wonderland', aware that she would eventually
awaken to a 'dull reality' (*Alice*, p. 163). But this awakening promises
a metamorphosis that is a teleological devolution: the 'rattling tea-
cups' degenerated into 'tinkling sheep-bells', the 'Queen's shrill cry'
declined into merely the 'voice of the shepherd boy', the odd
Wonderland noises settled into the form of the dull because overly
familiar farmyard 'clamour'. It is hard to miss both the note of
Romantic nostalgia for a lost experience of youth here as well as the
anti-Romantic repudiation of the sublimity of the pastoral: the sister
awakening from the vivid complexity of Alice's dream into the dull
'reality' of Wordsworth's rural visions.

Ultimately, *Alice's adventures in Wonderland* traces the defeat of the
diachronic form of comprehension that Hegel's philosophy promotes,
and does so in a way that constitutes one of the century's greatest
comic critiques of its ethnocentric premises. Because Alice fails to
successfully frame the events of her adventure, she must flee what has
become a nightmare, although that 'nightmare' is already being
recuperated by her sister at the end as a wonderful dream more vivid
than the dull life (which is really nothing but boring pastoral narrative, anyway) 'outside' that dream. One could observe that Alice's
inability to capture in her words to her sister the nightmarish quality
of her Wonderland adventures encourages that sister to recuperate the
narrative of the dream in a way that clearly falsifies it by sugar-coating
it, by, in effect, practising a bit of Alice's own highhanded imperial
reconstruction on us readers — another insidious kind of repetition
that, by now, can be seen for what it is. In this sense, Carroll may be

absolved of responsibility for the crime with which he has often been charged: the so-called 'crime' of attempting to insulate his readers from the far-reaching lessons of Alice's Wonderland dream by constructing a frame narrative which deliberately trivializes it. If anything, by suggesting that it is reconstructing the Wonderland dream under the guise of recapitulating it, the frame drives home the 'lesson' that there is a bit of the imperial Alice in all of us who engage in the twin activities of both 'comprehending' and 'repeating'.

As the most impressive comic critique of British ethnocentrism in the age of imperialism, Alice has a rightful claim to an important, if eccentric, place in the debate over the value of empire. A central assumption of Disraeli, Burton, and Kipling is an Hegelian one: one needs to 'know' the alien in order to know oneself; self-consciousness is dependent on other-consciousness. Thus, Tancred, A pilgrimage to El-Medinah and Mecca, and Kim plot a process of Bildung, of 'self-development' which occurs in proportion to the degree to which the 'subject' is able to impose a pattern of meaning on alien forms of life. This is an assumption which necessarily commits these authors to some degree of support for the political enterprise which ensures the availability and 'penetrability' of the alien field which supports the 'self', for the self, by this argument, is constructed out of the play of identities as the difference from those identities: the self needs the other for self-definition. Disraeli's works are governed by the logic of wish fulfilment. In his novels, the alien world (or the alien social class) is the privileged locus of the happy rediscovery of one's ancient claim to what one always thought one had to renounce in order to become an adult. To Burton, the Middle East offers essentially what India offers to Kim: a chance to don many masks, to reincarnate oneself many times; not to extinguish one's Englishness, but to look critically at what one is as an Englishman from the standpoint of the Other. Thus, Kim could not become Kim without pretending to be a whole series of people he is not. Nevertheless, despite Kipling's profound distaste for English conventionality, his book seems to reinforce the ethnocentric Victorian fiction of the individual; the opportunity and ability to don various masks seems to guarantee the existence of a self which dons masks, of a Kim who is Kim pretending to be someone else. As a tale of a little girl's arrested development, an anti-Bildungsroman, on the other hand, Alice in Wonderland insists on the ultimate indeterminacy of our knowledge of the other (and of the subject), of the way in which appropriation of his customs – indeed, understanding itself – is always a kind of falsification or misunderstanding. Consequently, in failing to comprehend the other, we, like Alice, remain ignorant of the subject which seeks to comprehend: unable to extract herself from the games which play her except by disrupting them, Alice is condemned to a cyclical plot of failed development. In short, in failing to be the 'Wise Man' in the drama of 'imperial' Bildung, one is condemned to play the 'master', and masters are bound to a state of arrested growth which is the consequence of their own failure to step outside the game of mastery to grasp its meaning.

Derrida argues that the science of anthropology begins in the nineteenth century as a critique of Western ethnocentrism. Indeed, one can see in the work of Burton (who, along with E. B. Tylor and A. C. Swinburne among others, was a member of Hunt's Anthropological Society, founded during the 1860s) a persistent compulsion to correct English misconceptions of the alien (to complement an even more persistent delight in puncturing middle-class Victorian moralism). More generally, one can see how the growing popular fascination with the primitive and exotic during the latter half of the century bespeaks a restless disenchantment with many aspects of conventional middle-class Victorian life. Yet this critical function of the interest in foreign cultures coexists with an imperial restiveness unprecedented in history. The critique of ethnocentrism grows apace with and, in fact, is fed by, as Said demonstrates, Western Europe's political incorporation of much of the rest of the globe: power and knowledge are wedded more closely to each other in the imperial field than anywhere else. The beauty of Alice in Wonderland lies in its minutely philosophical and enormously entertaining examination, in parable form, of precisely this historical paradox. Alice demonstrates that anthropological 'knowledge' of both the other and the self is both the issue at stake and a weapon in a political struggle for control. The 'winner' in such a contest has the last say about the meaning of cultural events, as Alice's sister can be held responsible for the generations of bowdlerized readings of Alice, readings which emphasize how 'wonderful' were Alice's adventures, ultimately responsible, in effect, for encouraging the cultural marginalization of Alice as 'delightful children's literature'.

Eight years after the Sepoy Mutiny, at a time when Britain was about to commit itself to an historically significant expansion of the formal institution of empire, during the period when Stanley's search for Livingstone would help to popularize the mythology of the imperialist as a benevolent explorer/missionary, filling in the blanks on the world map while bringing the benefits of 'Christianity and commerce' to brighten the dreary lives of the heathen, Carroll was reminding England of the fact that knowledge of the other is never disinterested but is often rather an aggressive reshaping of the unfamiliar to make it familiar, that the subject is never so clearly enclosed within his own ethnocentric walls as when he attempts to make sense of those who live in worlds radically different in fundamental respects from his own. While not an attack on imperialism as such, this reminder of just how extensively and profoundly culture and language shape – and ultimately distort – one's vision of other cultures is an important cautionary tale told to the children of an aggressively restless imperial power engaged in a political process of appropriation on a world-wide scale. It is ironically appropriate that an anti-Bildungsroman like Alice in Wonderland should end with the suggestion that even Alice, the aggressively conventional English girl of the Wonderland adventures, may be subject herself to the same kind of distortion at the hands of her simple-minded sister.

Moreover, while it may seem to be asking too much to insist that a 'children's' fantasy like Alice shoulder the heavy burden of these political implications, the example of Kim reminds us of the fact that the function which an author attributes to play commits him necessarily to a political position in the nineteenth century, and indeed, in our own. While the very fact that Kim was written testifies to Kipling's powers of sympathetic imagination and his grasp of the significance of cultural relativism – to be stateless and fatherless is to be attuned to the possibility of different interesting substitutions, to be 'decentred', free, as Disraeli's characters never are, of an ideological allegiance to that unifying centre that is the dream of the 'original' – it also reminds us of the important fact we have been underlining: that any true knowledge of the Other begins at the point where the subject extracts himself from the field on which he is imposing intellectual order, yet no such stance is attainable in a world in which the 'Wise Man' is always already implicated in the game of mastery. To Kipling's credit, he is willing to go far enough along the road to cultural relativism to construct his India as a circus of competing systems of meaning, although his need to master leads him to impose a 'harmonious' vision of the operation and reinforcement of empire by ultimately arresting that play at an arbitrary outer boundary, by, in effect, establishing the game of imperial management as the centre which, finally, controls and limits the play of substitution. Carroll, on the other hand, gives us a more 'honest' because more radical version of the failure of harmony, of the disharmony and conflict that characterize a world which refuses a little girl's attempt to master it by establishing herself as its centre: she who orders but somehow, magically, escapes being ordered herself. Wonderland, in other words, is a field of play that is not governed by a centre which can control the play of meanings, a world both less like our own than Kipling's is and more: a world offering more resistance to Alice's cultural imperialism than was, by and large, offered to Britain's in the nineteenth century, but a world that is, in the final analysis, ordered much like our own – solely by the exercise of force.

The 'civilized' in crisis

By the 1890s, the colonization of one-fourth of the world – the mission Disraeli, among others, defined in the 1870s – is on its way to completion, Britain having yet to face the crisis of confidence which the Boer War would precipitate. The effects of Britain's worldwide political dominance are being strongly felt in its literature, the public's insatiable taste for tales of imperial adventure in exotic locales bringing literary fame and fortune to a number of writers. The young Rudyard Kipling has taken literary London by storm with the publication of his Indian tales, G. A. Henty's books are recommended by most authorities on what children ought to read, H. Rider Haggard has become a popular writer almost on the scale of a Dickens, and Joseph Conrad has retired from the merchant navy to commit to paper his ambivalent response to the colonial enterprise.

In the post-Darwinian imperial age that is the late nineteenth century, 'knowledge' of the alien other is being produced on a large scale, and occasioning a crisis in the way England looks at itself. As Nietzsche notes, the discovery by reflective Europeans of other modes of living, alien cultural values which conflict with their own, cannot but provoke them to question the metaphysical sanction for their own values. Moreover, a heightened awareness of the 'problem of ethno-centrism', a theme explored in the second chapter here and an intellectual problematic which is the foundation of the field of anthropology,[1] nevertheless corresponds to a moment in English history when imperial appetites were at their most insatiable. The cultural paradox this might suggest – should not a growing cultural relativism have dampened English enthusiasm for conquest by causing men to question their assumption of superiority? – is only partially resolved by considering that the individuals who were most busily immersed in the project of extending the boundaries of the empire were either not, like Rhodes, worried about the impact of the European lust for new lands on indigenous populations, or, like Livingstone, concerned for the impact of European penetration on the native population but convinced that only extending the formal institution of the empire could offer them true protection from depradation.

As Savage argues, at this time the public taste for exciting, patriotic adventure coexisted with an interest in the customs of the exotic aliens whom Britain was conquering. While Haggard's Zulus play a conventional epic role as tragically heroic opponents of the British armies, their customs and way of life also exert a compelling interest for British readers who commonly frame these unfamiliar customs by assimilating them to the ways of English children, a class of beings with whom they rather too hastily assumed they were familiar. Already in the earlier part of the nineteenth century, as I have demonstrated, the Romantic intoxication with the 'original', which determines the plots of Disraeli's protagonists, suggests a loose analogy between the known and the unknown, Western childhood and alien ways of life. To move outward from the cultural centre is to move backwards in time. Moreover, as I have argued in Chapter 2, the later interest in imperial games evidenced in Burton, Carroll, and Kipling leads to the discovery that acculturation is enculturation: self-development hinges on learning strange cultural rules, a necessity requiring the development of a degree of cultural relativism with which Kim is blessed but which Alice fails to attain. Needless to say, the fact that both *Alice* and *Kim* trace the adventures of children is hardly accidental, for it is the child who faces the unenviable prospect of attempting to make sense of the world's games without the a priori security that a fully accomplished acculturation furnishes.

Nevertheless, the late nineteenth century is a time of crisis – epistemological, cultural, and historical – in which the metaphor of the child was to play a central role. The full implications of the Darwinian revolution were beginning to make themselves felt, and acceptance of the evolutionary hypothesis that all organic nature is ultimately one family raised a burning question requiring an historical explanation: if human beings were once beasts, whence comes that 'civilization' which Europeans claim as the crowning achievement which distinguishes them from beasts? This is the phylogenetic counterpart to the ontogenetic question of how the European individual becomes an 'imperial adult'.

As biology questioned the traditional religious belief that God intervened in worldly affairs to create man in his own image, the problem of accounting for the origin of that 'civilization' which Europeans were proud of exporting all over the world at this time naturally became acute. This is a question which did not seem to require a solution when God lay comfortingly behind the origin of human history. To Disraeli's generation, of course, Genesis accounted both for the social reality of imperfection and sin and for the fondly cherished hope in human perfectibility. Thus, Tancred constructs his empire in the confidence that comes of possessing the book of world history; moreover, the Romantic historical myth which posits adulthood as a kind of 'fall' from an aboriginal childhood, the secular myth which underpins Tancred's adventure, is an obvious parallel to this biblical myth. As Disraeli's predecessors Wordsworth and the Romantics raised 'childhood' to an historically new position of intellectual and imaginative prominence earlier in the century, evolutionary theory performed a similar service for the 'primitive', which, by the end of the century, was coming to be seen as holding the key to the mysterious origins of the 'modern' or 'civilized'. Where Wordsworth's Immortality Ode defined adulthood as a state of recognizing what one lost in the transition from childhood; the 'modern' or 'civilized', in the works of such writers as Haggard and Lang, was coming to be defined as the state of experiencing the loss of one's 'primitiveness', a rupture with the past which condemns one to return to the primitive world of the present to recover one's bearings. Needless to say, such a return can never be politically innocent, as it was not innocent in Disraeli's day, for the privilege of returning is often only enabled by the existence of world-wide European empires and the self-confident proprietary attitudes which they engender.

By the end of the century, evolutionary modes of thought and the questions they raised have had a wide influence. Those seeking to read alien ways of life for the light they cast on the 'childhood' of the English race are guided in doing so by the tenets of Evolutionary Anthropology. E. B. Tylor's Primitive culture, published in 1871, is recognized as the standard work in this newly important field, and Sir James Frazer's magnum opus, The golden bough, destined to exert an enormous influence in the early twentieth century, is in the process of being released in the 1890s. In fact, the field of Evolutionary Anthropology crossed a watershed of intellectual respectability when Tylor himself was appointed to the first chair of Anthropology at Oxford in 1896.

What I am suggesting is that notions of the 'barbaric', the 'uncivilized', the 'primitive', the 'childlike', the alien in time and the alien in space overlap constantly in the Victorian imagination of the late nineteenth century, blurring distinctions which some in the twentieth century will later erect between phylogeny and ontogeny, cultural evolution and individual development, the history of the 'race' and the history of the individual, the customs of the primitive and the behaviour of Western children. But at the time, Evolutionary Anthropology offered a compelling hypothesis which promised to bring system and order to conceptions of seemingly disparate phenomena. Much like the earlier 'Great Chain of Being', this single evolutionary scale of development holds out a promise of total coherence too tantalizing to be dismissed. Moreover, as with all global explanatory hypotheses, the purely analogical relationships eventually begin to be broken down into more literal ones as, in circular fashion, anthropologists draw on their knowledge of childhood to illuminate the primitive and psychologists consult their reading of anthropological accounts of the primitive to explain childhood: thus, for example, Andrew Lang draws on a commonly-held fund of knowledge about childhood to explain the behaviour of primitive tribesmen, while Freud later raids the anthropological literature on primitives for insight into the psychic lives of neurotics and children.[2]

Although the equation of the childlike and the primitive was common at the turn of the century, and, indeed, still haunts the modern Western view of the 'underdeveloped world',[3] three writers (Haggard, Conrad, and Hardy) are central to the discussion here because in their work they go well beyond a simple-minded recapitulation of the Victorian cultural hierarchy of the civilized over the primitive. All three self-consciously draw on evolutionary ideas to define the 'civilized' as existing in a multifarious dependency relationship with the 'primitive', a relationship which they could explore not only because evolutionary doctrines had brought these two realms together, but because political imperialism was making 'available' to Europeans the lives and customs of existent 'primitives' and, in Hardy's case, suggesting analogies between 'primitive' aliens and England's homegrown 'primitives'. Empire, in short, seemed like a relatively convenient laboratory for the study of the childhood of the world.

For these three writers, historical return is a hazardous albeit necessary adventure which inevitably raises important questions about the relationship between the past one thinks one has surmounted and the present which enables one to reconstruct that past. In Haggard, for instance, the primitive is dislocated from its conventional opposition to the civilized and placed in a new relationship with the civilized as its heretofore unknown maternal origin, but an origin which must then be carefully sealed off from the present. Conrad takes greater risks: his Congo cannot be sealed off at the end of *Heart of darkness* to protect England from contamination, as Haggard seals off the cave in which 'She-Who-Must-Be-Obeyed' takes her final fire-bath, for the same water which flows into the heart of darkness flows up the Thames, making England also 'one of the dark places of the earth'.[4] Conrad's novel is preoccupied with the fluid boundary between the civilized and the primitive.

Most importantly, Hardy's *Jude* merits discussion here because of Hardy's novel artistic translation of the conflict between civilization and the primitive to England itself, and the conclusions to which this leads him: his rejection of the 'restorative' mission of history, the mission which underlay Disraeli's metahistorical thesis. To Hardy, finally, this restorative or reparative mission of history is illusory: 'civilization' needs the 'primitive' as its other, existing in a state of permanent exteriority, both to protect itself from contamination and to define its 'civilization' by opposition to the 'primitive' – the 'primitive' in Hardy becomes, finally, a cultural unconscious. The gap between the two cannot be bridged, as Disraeli's metahistorical myth proposes, without collapsing the civilized into the primitive. Thus Hardy articulates a contradictory vision which stresses the impossibility of reconciling these two domains and the necessity of perpetual antagonism. His relationship to the surmounted 'primitive' past is not at all a simple romantic nostalgia for a past frozen forever into perpetual marginal existence in rural England, but rather a complexly contradictory attitude that locates the tragic nature of human life in the coexistence of change and continuity, the historical reality of irrecoverable loss of the primitive past with the sense that the past is forever repeating itself in the present, a deeply felt sense of regret co-existing with the conviction that nothing is finally lost – an unstable intellectual position which Nietzsche would attempt to stabilize by inventing the problematic myth of 'Eternal Recurrence' and which Freud would later engage by comparing the psyche to a 'Mystic Writing-Pad'.[5]

Where Edmund Burke in the eighteenth century had confidently defined civilization as what savagery is not, the late nineteenth century, and none in more illuminating fashion than Hardy, tried to find a model for accommodating both the tension of this conventional opposition and the profound implications in the newly undeniable 'fact' emphasized by late Victorian science – that the savage is the mother of the civilized.

II

While a popular jingoist writer like Henty offers the standard delights of the epic celebration of masculine heroism (*With Clive in India*, for instance), Haggard's novels use the imperial setting to tap a level of yearning which, by contrast, seems almost indecent in its disregard for the standards of middle-class Victorian behaviour. By sexualizing the landscape of darkest Africa as he does (for instance, his unsubtle metaphorization of the African landscape as a female body inviting male penetration: both in *She*, 1888, and in his first novel *King Solomon's mines*, 1885) and surrounding it with a veil of barely disguised mystery which the West must draw aside, Haggard adopts the Romantic theme of return to the original but repositions it within the 'primitive' world as the late nineteenth century conceived it.[6] 'Darkest Africa' becomes the locus of adventure and initiation where otherwise 'civilized' Englishmen must go in order to complete themselves. To Haggard, civilization is somehow incomplete: it is an orphan state. As the motherless Vincey discovers, re-establishing one's connection with the world, one's genealogy, requires delving into an arena of tropical fertility where the past persists in the present – in this case, the 'primitive' world of sub-Saharan Africa.

Thus, in his overdetermined description of a lost kingdom located somewhere in central Africa, a description for which he seems to have been greatly indebted to Disraeli's depiction of the lost realm of the Queen of the Ansarey in *Tancred*, Haggard metaphorizes She as the sexualized mother of 'us' all, the rediscovered Eve embodying subterranean fecundity, magical powers, brutal savagery, and historical decadence in unholy combination. Moreover, by locating her city in the midst of the central African jungle, inspired by the contemporary discovery of the ruins of the ancient African kingdom of Zimbabwe, Haggard employs an anomalous figure which is structured by the logic of the supplement: both 'savage' and 'civilized' at the same time, Kôr is a fitting abode for a woman who embodies Haggard's ambivalence toward both savagery and civilization. If contemporary theory required a 'missing link' in the evolutionary chain of the species, combining anomalously the features of both the bestial and the human, then cultural evolution required an historically analogous 'missing society', holding in unholy tension the features of savage social existence and modern civilized life. This is Kôr.

When She takes her fire bath at the end of the novel and reverts to an aged child/monkey, her ontogenetic and phylogenetic regression is at once a typical moral influenced by the 'pessimistic' tradition of cultural regression (the Duke of Argyll thesis) and an unwelcome authorial punishment meted out to the unwitting male reader who has been encouraged to develop an unwholesome interest in the sexually enticing She over the course of the novel.[7] She's reversion, thus, produces the necessary disgust for the past (by showing its evolutionarily 'lower' features), a disgust which reasserts a sufficiently comfortable separation between the modern English adventurers Holly and Vincey and the ancient 'source' which She represents (a separation paradoxically threatened throughout most of the novel). Meanwhile, Haggard also reinforces aesthetically the prohibition against return and regression: recoiling from She in disgust, Holly and Vincey can then surmount their temptation to follow her back to the womb, the familiar temptation of the cyclical plot, the temptation of incest. Thus, Holly learns the common English novelistic lesson that 'true love' requires renunciation of the original, a lesson familiar from Disraeli's treatment of the imperial hero, and Haggard commits his heroes to mortality and the linear plot of imperial heroism by sealing the cavern at the end (She, p. 293).

Although Haggard's protagonists, like Disraeli's, are driven by an interest in returning to the origins of history, between the writing of Tancred and She the full flowering of Darwinism intervened to ensure that the latter book confronts more graphically the dangers – and, conversely, the libidinal pleasures – lurking in cultural and psychological regression. Both sets of heroes confront the attractions and the dangers of a return through history. However, the origin to which Holly and Vincey return is imaginatively drawn from a synthesis of late nineteenth-century cultural diffusionist theories which locate the source of world civilizations, not in the relatively familiar "biblicized" Middle East of Disraeli's generation, but in the centre of the mysterious unknown – Africa – and near the source of the river which was the lifeblood of the first great civilization known to Europeans at the time – Egypt.[8]

By Haggard's time, evolutionary theory had encouraged the inference that the beginnings of human history date back hundreds of thousands of years to a point at which human life emerges almost imperceptibly from the continuum of animal life. In *She*, Haggard reformulates the Disraelian point that the harrowing of the primitive world is somehow an essential initiation rite for English gentlemen: one must return to a land which lies at the beginning of history to purchase a necessary fresh perspective on modern English life, but like the prohibited return to the mother, one finds that the law which establishes 'civilization', the law which separates 'civilized' man from the animals or savages, also prohibits such a return.

Unlike Tancred's Eva, the Siren-like She ultimately represents the promise not of return to some Golden Age Eden before the Fall, as she claims, but of return to an ignominious kinship with lower species, a bridging of what had been a yawning gulf until Darwin's time, boldly represented to Holly and Vincey by her startling reversion to the aged child/monkey. One can thus see Haggard's overdetermined descriptions of the ancient world of Kôr also as attempts to purchase a distance from this threatening world which is necessarily part of Europe's own past. Thus, Vincey, an orphan in England, begins his adventure with the discovery of his own descent from Kallikrates, the priest of Isis: his voyage to Africa represents an attempt to restore himself to his own family, to re-establish his links with his genealogical past – a necessary stage in his own self-development but hardly one to which he initially looks forward with unalloyed delight. Nevertheless, one could say that European man could risk succumbing to the lure of the 'primitive' in the late nineteenth century partly because he was so well armoured against its dangers. Having established 'scientifically' the disturbing fact of kinship with the savage, Evolutionary Anthropology offered the means of framing 'savage' customs to protect Europeans against the threat that this kinship represented.

The most noteworthy 'defence' of this sort was the doctrine of 'survivals'. A 'survival', according to E. B. Tylor who is most closely associated with this doctrine, is any feature of a more 'primitive' stage of society which persists in a more 'advanced' society, without serving any function. As Burrow argues, '"The theory of survivals" encouraged men to see parallels between primitive and civilized practices, but it drew the sting and the stimulus from the comparison by regarding the former as relics, aliens from another era. It seemed to broaden horizons, but in fact it was a device for keeping them in the same place. The epithet which naturally accompanies "survivals" is "mere"'.[9] Like the analogy between the 'savage' and the child, it both expresses the kinship between the 'modern' and the 'primitive' which modern science requires one to acknowledge while also placing the latter at a safe distance, in a container marked heavily with the warning labels 'different', 'inferior', and 'irrational'.

Thus, the doctrine of survivals codified cultural ambivalence about the connection between the modern and the distant evolutionary past in an era in which historical return was fraught with implications even more frightful than the incest and miscegenation threats which preoccupied Disraeli. To label a cultural feature a 'survival' is to project oneself safely outside the culture in which it once, presumably, had a function in order to appropriate it in its alienation, to 'know' it as a 'survival'. The survival is by definition non-functional; it represents the evolutionary past which he who studies it has, necessarily, surmounted. The ethnographer who studies survivals thus places himself in a position analogous to that of the Hegelian 'Wise Man': he frames the meaning of strange cultural events from the privileged position of detached rational outsider, claiming a unique freedom from the distortions which bedevil those who try to understand from within a master/slave game. As *Alice* reminds, however, the 'master's' belief that he is really the 'Wise Man' in the game of cultural difference is the ultimate imperial fiction.

Nevertheless, lest we forget what an 'advance' this doctrine represented, we should emphasize the way in which it also implicated nineteenth-century England in an historical kinship with the savage tribes it sought to exploit. Thus, from the 1890s on, it is no longer quite as easy as it had been for a well-read Englishman to feel the kind of absolute superiority to the savage which he might have felt in the 1860s, for, after all, the Eucharist his local bishop celebrates at the Cathedral of a Sunday might well contain traces of a more primitive sacrificial ritual from which it once derived. In fact, the enormous influence of Frazer's *Golden bough* (as well as the reactions of outrage it provoked) had much to do with precisely this historical relationship he implied between the Christian ritual of symbolic sacrifice and a more ancient practice of king-murder – its savage progenitor. The savage past of humanity persists in the present, although it represents itself in a way that, many feared, threatened to contaminate the 'highest' features of European civilization.

D

She ends with an attempt at eliminating this threat of the primitive living on into the present: not only does the author kill off She, but, in sealing off the cave, Haggard's heroes rupture the connection between past and present, the mother of world cultures and her progeny, which the novel has, ironically, tried to re-establish. However, this last scene cannot avoid insinuating that Holly and Vincey are also undergoing a kind of rebirth out of the last of the many womb structures (the cave) which the novel presents, thus hinting at Haggard's ambivalence about this repression of the connection between past and present, the primitive origin and its civilized progeny. Haggard's entombment of the dead past is ultimately novelistically unsatisfactory because it is an act of repression carried out in the face of all of his hard novelistic work at making the past look attractive: the sexualized mother must – for obvious psychological and ethical reasons – be repudiated. However, despite his best effort at creating a revulsion from the primitive past by representing it through She's reversion to an aged monkey, Haggard finally cannot repudiate it completely. He can only contain that past safely where, he hopes, it will not contaminate the present, tabooing it by safely enfolding it within another womb – the narrative that is the story of his heroes' adventures. This act of entombing the past (veiling the sexual mystery) is paralleled in that other narrative, the reading of which led them to Kôr in the first place, the story within a story salvaged from an Egyptian casket and containing Vincey's genealogy and revealing his destiny as a matricide.[10] However, as the existence of the strong-box and its papers merely fuel the heroes' curiosity in the beginning of the book, She's association with Egyptian practices of mummification and her final entombment suggest that by the end Haggard's heroes have only restored the conditions of enticing mystery which existed at the beginning of the novel, that She's mystery has again been secreted in another kind of strong-box, ever ready to lure new adventurers to return to Africa, remove the rock, and disclose the forbidden mysteries of cultural origins. The entombment of the past simply reinstates the conditions of enticing mystery extant at the beginning.

In *Heart of darkness* (1899), Conrad also evokes the necessity of return to the 'first ages', but does so without either affirming the mission of the Disraelian imperial hero who must recapitulate a familiarized past or Haggard's imperial hero as repudiator of an attractive past. In fact, the term 'hero' carries a dual meaning in much of Conrad's fiction, because his fiction foregrounds the Hegelian structure of imperial incorporation, the ambiguous interplay between 'master' and 'Wise Man'.

In *Heart of darkness*, Kurtz's plight, the plight of the tragic hero/ imperial agent, is recapitulated in Marlow's narrative of his own adventures: neither the role of god (Kurtz) nor that of story-teller (Marlow) guarantees one a privileged position as 'Wise Man', for the imperial experience menaces the distinction between inside and outside which founds the difference between 'knower' and 'actor', 'Wise Man' and 'master'. Kurtz's failure to extract himself from his role as god in order to see his actions with a degree of detachment – to climb out of his megalomaniacal trap – is paralleled with Marlow's failure to 'explain' Kurtz's tragic heroism. This collapse is both a threat posed by cultural regression and a tragic insight into the human condition conferred by cultural relativism, and thus, something to which the other, more pedestrian, company men are blind. In other words, the form of Conrad's narrative, his focusing of his narrative through the words of Marlow, may well be a 'psychologization' – in effect, a 'privatization' – of the 'political' imperial experience, protecting English readers from being fully implicated in empire by rendering it in the terms of a psychological drama,[11] but it also enmeshes the teller of the tale – Marlow – in a transferential relationship with Kurtz that is the psychological analogue of the political experience of loss of boundaries: as Kurtz's power game is played out in the jungle of the Congo with the Russian and the native Africans, Marlow exercises his power by manipulating his own listeners (and readers).

However, this demonstrates not so much Conrad's desperate defence against the political ramifications of empire, but rather his ability to appreciate how Europe's attempt to produce a discourse on empire mires it in a transferential quagmire. To affirm a relationship with the past, the savage, the alien, that is one of both opposition and filiation requires one to construct a model which will satisfactorily countenance the aporia of that dual relationship: a model for which Hegel's dialectic, with its almost mystical notion of 'synthesis', is inadequate, but one which will later be furnished for the twentieth century in Freud's notion of the 'unconscious'.

Thus, as Marlow reveals, Kurtz is 'larger than life' in both the heroic sense and the megalomaniacal sense because he dares to risk the boundaries of the self in the wilderness:

He had taken a high seat amongst the devils of the land – I mean literally. You can't understand. How could you? – with solid pavement under your feet, surrounded by kind neighbours ready to cheer you or to fall on you, stepping delicately between the butcher and the policeman, in the holy terror of scandal and gallows and lunatic asylums – how can you imagine what particular region of the first ages a man's untrammelled feet may take him into by the way of solitude – utter solitude without a policeman – by the way of silence – utter silence, where no warning voice of a kind neighbour can be heard whispering of public opinion? (*Heart of darkness*, p. 50)

Living among familiar surroundings is what guarantees the distinction between interior and exterior, the self and the world. It makes the world 'comprehensible' by allowing it to be framed and marked off from the self. As the familiarity of the environment conditions the unexpectedly 'civilized restraint' of the 'cannibals' on Marlow's boat, so a lack of familiar surroundings conditions the failure of Kurtz's humanity upriver. Living amidst completely alien surroundings – cultural and physical – in the Congo, Kurtz experiences the loss of exteriority and thus of the bounds of the self. He becomes a megalomaniacal ruler-god but also a tragic hero because he dares to harrow the hell of total appropriation: a state in which all becomes the self because all is unfamiliar but also pliable, manipulable. In Marlow's view, only the familiar offers resistance to appropriation, and thus, places 'restraints' upon the imperial self.[12] Living 'in the midst of the incomprehensible' is necessarily 'detestable' because one cannot know whether what one detests is oneself or one's environment. Kurtz is surrounded by slaves – including the Russian who toadies to him shamelessly out of abject fear – whose recognition he desires, whose resistance he will not brook, and whose company, ironically, merely intensifies his solitude.[13] The heads on pikes turned inward towards his compound suggest the ultimately unsatisfying dilemma his imperial mastery creates for him: recognition converted to empty gesture.

Conrad establishes the dualistic relationship between Marlow and Kurtz in order to tell two stories of return to the 'first ages': one (Marlow's) narrated after it has presumably already occurred and one (Kurtz's) that can be reconstructed only by inference, one which purports to be the story of overcoming the lure of 'savagery' by opting out of the game of mastery and one which is an ironic lesson in how playing the master converts one into a slave to brutal instincts. Marlow's narration of his journey up the river merely hints at where

Kurtz succumbed to the lure of the primitive by having Marlow tell us, in self-congratulatory fashion, how he surmounted it. Where Kurtz, the representative of the best of European civilization, succumbs to the imperative to play the master to impose a morally ambiguous order on a darkness, Marlow preserves his bounded self in Hegelian fashion, so he tells us, by playing the proletarian bound to the saving doctrine of work:

There were moments when one's past came back to one, as it will sometimes when you have not a moment to spare to yourself; but it came in the shape of an unrestful and noisy dream, remembered with wonder amongst the overwhelming realities of this strange world of plants, and water, and silence. And this stillness of life did not in the least resemble a peace. It was the stillness of an implacable force brooding over an inscrutable intention. It looked at you with a vengeful aspect. I got used to it afterwards; I did not see it any more; I had no time. I had to keep guessing at the channel; I had to discern, mostly by inspiration, the signs of hidden banks; I watched for sunken stones; I was learning to clap my teeth smartly before my heart flew out, when I shaved by a fluke some infernal sly old snag that would have ripped the life out of the tin-pot steamboat and drowned all the pilgrims; I had to keep a look-out for the signs of dead wood we could cut up in the night for next day's steaming. When you have to attend to things of that sort, to the mere incidents of the surface, the reality – the reality, I tell you – fades. The inner truth is hidden – luckily, luckily. (*Heart of darkness*, p. 34)

Thus, work on a familiar object – the ship – engaged in a familiar task – piloting upriver – is what saves Marlow from the fate that engulfs Kurtz – so he thinks. In Hegelian terms, the boat represents for Marlow both his own labour in restoring it to floatable condition ('objectified subjectivity') and a principle of resistance to his efforts to keep it afloat, a resistance which teaches him a lesson about the boundaries of his self, a lesson which the too-compliant natives at Kurtz's station presumably do not teach him because they worship him as a god.[14] Thus, the key to Marlow's value of 'restraint' seems to lie both in resistance – in his case, the resistance that dead matter makes to his own effort to shape it to his purposes – and self-referential familiarity – the recognition of his own infusion of subjectivity into the object, his identifying the traces of his own handiwork in the rivets which hold the boat together. Moreover, it would not be going too far to say that in death Kurtz becomes Marlow's steamboat, in effect, a legend which accepts Marlow's infusion of his own tragic overtones but which resists his attempt to make him heroic in a morally unalloyed way.

In effect, Marlow's gospel of work is his way of staying afloat, of retaining his hold on enough of the familiar world to avoid Kurtz's fate, but at the cost of acknowledging himself a lesser man than Kurtz ('disciple' rather than 'master'). If the master's prime illusion is mastery, then Marlow avoids that trap by becoming the spokesman for the ('slavish') idea that the 'primitive' cannot be mastered but only – occasionally – evaded. Discussing the meaning of the wilderness in Africa, he hints that return to the 'first ages' of time, the 'wilderness' of human history, is an experience that, in contrast to Haggard's narrative, does not lead to development, growth, or maturity through an act of constitutive repression, a taming of the brutal environment and the inner brutality of the self. Speaking of the Romans who first tackled the wilderness that was savage Britain, he asks his listeners to imagine a young Roman,

Land in a swamp, march through the woods, and in some inland post feel the savagery, the utter savagery, had closed round him – all that mysterious life of the wilderness that stirs in the forest, in the jungles, in the hearts of wild men. There's no initiation either into such mysteries. He has to live in the midst of the incomprehensible, which is also detestable. And it has a fascination, too, that goes to work upon him. The fascination of the abomination – you know. Imagine the growing regrets, the longing to escape, the powerless disgust, the surrender, the hate. (*Heart of darkness*, p. 6)

This is an anticipation of Kurtz meant to prepare us for seeing him cast in a sympathetic light. The breakdown of the inside/outside distinction is perfectly rendered here in Marlow's description of a young man 'living in the midst of the incomprehensible', a state of being which denies one mastery by denying one the opportunity to erect boundaries to 'comprehend'. Even the wilderness exists both 'out there' and inside the 'hearts' of men, as Kurtz's final judgement ('The horror! The horror!') is at least as much a judgement of himself as of Africa.

Conrad not only raises questions about the traditional European assumption of innate superiority here (by locating 'civilization' simply in the arbitrary historical accident of superior force), but this difference he establishes between Marlow and Kurtz suggests that he has complicated the Hegelian 'master'/'Wise Man' dichotomy that we have discussed earlier. While Marlow seems to avoid the extreme megalomania which afflicts Kurtz, he does not thereby become the 'Wise Man', as the elusive nature of the language he uses to sum up the meaning of Kurtz's experience indicates he cannot get 'outside'

his struggle with him to frame Kurtz effectively, even though the
conventional authoritative role of the narrator seems to condition his
readers (and listeners) to expect that of him. That Marlow is engaged
in a transferential game with Kurtz – at once attempting to
comprehend and convey the meaning of the life of this man with
whom he has struggled and has sworn to serve – is revealed in a
number of places in the narrative. One sees this when Marlow is forced
to play master – such as when he prevents the sickly Kurtz, regressively
crawling on all fours, from rousing the natives against the whites at
his station. But, in death, this power relationship seems to be reversed:
Kurtz achieves an ascendancy over Marlow which is revealed in
Marlow's claim that he is his 'last disciple', suggesting he accepts his
subordination somewhat uncritically, and perhaps, that the 'truth'
lying behind his entire narrative celebration of Kurtz is tainted by the
slavish acceptance of the necessity to serve him – that, in effect,
Marlow's narrativization of Kurtz is an act of 'colonial mimicry'.
Moreover, Conrad returns to the frame occasionally to reinforce
parallels between Marlow (the 'idol') and Kurtz (the false god) which
elaborate the transference, the uncanny interchangeability of Marlow
and Kurtz. He follows, for instance, Marlow's description of Kurtz as
nothing but a disembodied voice with a return to the frame which
ironically emphasizes both Marlow's voice and his own disembodi-
ment. Having just described how he imagined Kurtz simply as a
disembodied voice – pure discourse ('I made the strange discovery
that I had never imagined him as doing, you know, but as
discoursing', Heart of darkness, p. 48) – and, moreover, emitting a
morally ambiguous discourse which is at once a 'pulsating stream of
light' and a 'deceitful glow from the heart of an impenetrable
darkness', Marlow the storyteller is then described by the frame:

There was a pause of profound stillness, then a match flared, and Marlow's
lean face appeared, worn, hollow, with downward folds and dropped eyelids,
with an aspect of concentrated attention; and as he took vigorous draws at
his pipe, it seemed to retreat and advance out of the night in the regular flicker
of the tiny flame. (Heart of darkness, p. 48)

The frame cements the parallel here between Marlow and Kurtz by
recapitulating Kurtz's anomalous ontological status in Marlow's
indeterminate 'presence'. Like the earlier description of Marlow as an
'idol' and the echoes of Kurtz's own hollowness in the use of the word
'hollow' here, the novel not only undermines Marlow's narrative
authority by paralleling him with the figure he should be compre-

hending and explaining to us, but it calls into question whether or not Marlow has ever truly returned from the heart of darkness, has ever achieved a position from which he can comprehend Kurtz by standing outside him, can ever, in short, render the numinous 'reality' of Kurtz through the hollow signifiers of his own discourse. This passage, and others in which he uses words as ironic weapons against his listeners suggest, at least, that he cannot.

Perhaps this is why Marlow is ultimately condemned to affirm the value of the idolatry he practises, to contribute to enhancing the myth of Kurtz when he lies about Kurtz's last words to his Intended. In fact, what Marlow seems most to appreciate about Kurtz is – not surprisingly – what he most appreciated in himself: his power as word-giver, his ability to articulate the darkness, to give form to the unformed, to differentiate the undifferentiated with words, to judge, particularly if the one he judges is himself:

He had summed up – he had judged. 'The horror!' He was a remarkable man. After all, this was the expression of some sort of belief; it had candour, it had conviction, it had a vibrating note of revolt in its whisper, it had the appalling face of a glimpsed truth – the strange commingling of desire and hate. (*Heart of darkness*, p. 72)

Of course, Marlow's explanation here suggests a purely aesthetic or formalist appreciation of Kurtz: regardless of whether his judgement is appropriate or 'true', Marlow argues, Kurtz gives the appearance of believing it, and belief, because it fills a void, because it is a creative substitute for the hollowness at the core of life, or rather, because it is a way of papering over the contradictory nature of life implied by the 'strange commingling of desire and hate', is worthwhile in itself. If Marlow comes to worship Kurtz, he does so only in the conscious realization that he is worshipping an idol, yet idolatry, he argues, is absolutely necessary for creating the values by which everyone must live.[15] Even imperialism itself, the 'idea' of imperialism, is a form of necessary idolatry, as he reveals early in the novel:

It was just robbery with violence, aggravated murder on a great scale, and men going at it blind – as is very proper for those who tackle a darkness. The conquest of the earth, which mostly means the taking it away from those who have a different complexion or slightly flatter noses than ourselves, is not a pretty thing when you look into it too much. What redeems it is the idea only. An idea at the back of it; not a sentimental pretence but an idea; and an unselfish belief in the idea – something you can set up, and bow down before, and offer a sacrifice to . . . . (*Heart of darkness*, p. 7)

In this revelation, which purports to be measured observation, the fruit of long and sorry experience, but which we later come to see also as bald self-justification, Marlow reveals his own allegiance to a survival of primitivism which he refuses to relinquish because he finds it conjoined with the highest values of Western culture: like fetishism, idolatry – the worship of false gods, the celebration of the 'sensible' reality of the signifier at the expense of the merely 'intelligible' signified it only represents, of the word as word, of value for the sake of any value – would be immediately recognized by any Victorian as a survival of a 'primitive' stage of cultural development. Yet here it is affirmed by a modern who has self-confessedly evolved beyond the worship of conventional idols to the worship of the idea of idolatry itself – in the full light of all the horror of such hollow belief as well as its good. Marlow's idolatry of Kurtz, his claim to be his last disciple, is a sign of his paradoxical regression to a new and higher stage of development. That there is no higher synthesis to attain here, that Marlow finally reverts to serving the memory of the white-faced invalid he found crawling on all fours in the jungle, as his journey up the river to retrieve Kurtz conveniently serves the interests of the company he deplores, reveals Conrad's doubts about the possibility of mastery of the primitive past which is opened up by a political enterprise which is both deplorable exploitation and a necessary descent into a hell which has not yet been subdivided into the neat categories – the unconscious, the past, primitive life – by which the twentieth century articulates the darkness, a hell which the romance conventions of Western 'heroism' can still be called upon to structure (Jameson, p. 267).

Although Marlow recognizes that only holding on to the familiar preserves one from succumbing to Kurtz's style of megalomania, that realization offers him little hope of ultimate mastery, for, as the novel make quite clear, the 'primitive' is merely an elastic label one applies to the other, the unfamiliar, the world which defies conventional classification. Moreover, as the case of Kurtz demonstrates, that 'other' is also the self. In such a Nietzschean world, the values one identifies with the 'civilized' are nothing more than those which have been appropriated as one's own: a realization which subverts the conventional hierarchy of the civilized over the primitive by removing its metaphysical sanction. What the imperial enterprise opens up, in Conrad's view, is the frightening prospect not simply of a confrontation with one's forgotten self returned to one in its alienation but of the even more harrowing inability to control this confrontation, to shape it in a way that preserves the separation between shaper and shaped. One might say that the ambiguously incomplete relation of separation between the mother and the child she carries in her womb, master and slave, civilized and primitive, is the fear which the male power to generate words is called to alleviate here. Unlike the phallic heroes of Haggard's story who wall up the female power of the primitive in a gesture which is simultaneously a repudiation of the womb from which they themselves once sprung and a re-establishment of the separation between past and present, mother and children, the primitive and the civilized – an almost pathetic attempt to contain by distancing the enormous generative power of the earth – Conrad's Marlow tells a tale in which the power of words to give shape to the shapeless hollowness of existence is celebrated while it is simultaneously revealed as the manufacture of lies. That Marlow cannot utter a word about Kurtz the manufacturer of discourse which is not also an oblique way of congratulating himself for being such a vividly impressive story-teller, reveals that Marlow himself has been swallowed up in a 'darkness' that is not so much "out there" as it is enveloping the whole enterprise of imperial mastery.

III

During the latter part of the nineteenth century, the imaginative possibilities stimulated by the notion of 'survivals' precipitated a search for the evidence of the 'druidic' and 'Germanic' past of England – the alien but homegrown past – which would help identify Thomas Hardy with a growing popular nostalgia for a pre-industrial 'Old England'.[16] During the Romantic period, Scott's historical novels initiated the modern celebration of a romanticized medieval England, while, during the Victorian age, the Pre-Raphaelites, Ruskin, Morris, and Tennyson helped to authorize tearful regret for the passing of a rural way of life identified with the distant English past of legend. However, despite his popular reputation, Hardy used the past in a novel way in his fiction: in Hardy, the past does not simply irrupt into the present with devastating consequences. *Jude the obscure*, arguably the most complex of Hardy's novels, is a tale of struggle between the 'primitive' past and modern 'civilization', a struggle which the former is destined to lose in one sense – the rural lower classes which Jude represents are an economic and social atavism by the 1890s – and win in another – the novel foregrounds a cultural 'repetition compulsion' in which repression of the past condemns one to repeat it. Moreover, Hardy is the one English writer of the late nineteenth century to fully examine in his fiction the significantly subversive effect of rapid historical change in the present: he depicts a society in the act of producing 'survivals' at an alarming rate, a society committed to colonizing its rural lower classes as it is colonizing the dark races of the world, and moving at a rapid pace to convert the past into the present so that it may be safely stowed away where it can no longer threaten the present.

That said, it is important to note that *Jude* is not a classic Victorian social novel like *North and South*, at least in part because Hardy does not represent here a conflict of industrial classes. Rather he poses an opposition between a cultural ideal that unifies power and knowledge (Christminster) and a representative of a past which has no place in the present (Marygreen), a particular way of appropriating the past from outside it (Christminster's) against a knowledge of the past which can only come from living within it (Marygreen's).

In all his later fiction, Hardy evokes the popular evolutionary scale of cultural development to account for the persistence of the ancient customs and way of life of the rural lower classes in England, a class of whose imminent demise he is the chief chronicler.[17] Thus, one is not surprised to find him quoting with approval, in his *Life*, his banker friend Clodd's explanation of why the 'superstitions' of an 'Asiatic' and a 'Dorset labourer' are the same:

Dec. 18. Mr. E. Clodd this morning gives an excellently neat answer to my question why the superstitions of a remote Asiatic and a Dorset labourer are the same; – 'The attitude of man,' he says, 'at corresponding levels of culture, before like phenomena, is pretty much the same, your Dorset peasants representing the persistence of the barbaric idea which confuses persons and things, and founds wide generalizations on the slenderest analogies.'[18]

As Clodd explains, this kind of 'confusion' of 'persons and things' is typical of children, a point which he 'proves' at great length in his book *The childhood of the world* (1878).[19]

Unlike Haggard and Conrad, Hardy displaces within England itself the process of exteriorization and appropriation which is at the heart of the new relationship to the primitive at the end of the century. Jude himself, like the social class into which he was born, is a 'survival': a medieval craftsman surviving into the nineteenth century but ill-fitted for life in a new class-based social structure.[20] However, Hardy's final judgement on him is very incompletely rendered by the term 'mere survival'. Jude draws its initial strength from evolutionary notions but then sails well beyond them to arrive at an uncharted shore, bereft of the hope that 'evolutionary meliorism' afforded many of his contemporaries. Jude should be read not simply as a parable of the rise and fall of an individual 'medieval' craftsman in the nineteenth century, a social novel dramatizing the inevitable disappointment of the main character's hope of surmounting the class barriers condemning him to poverty and 'obscurity', but as a parable of the rise of England out of and then the subsequent fall back into a kind of primeval barbarism, an empowerment of consciousness which appropriates realms of the unconscious only to seek its own destruction in a return to unconsciousness. Jude is both an exteriorized victim of a social process of exclusion, a member of an atavistic social group begging admittance into the modern England of knowledge and power which Christminster represents metonymically, and a representative figure who recapitulates in his own plot a repression of the past analogous to that which Christminster perpetrates against him. Both perpetrator and victim simultaneously, Jude much more closely resembles Kurtz than Haggard's imperial heroes in his freedom from radical innocence, and thus, through this character, Hardy is able to demonstrate how the civilizing process entails both radical deracination and the inevitable return of the repressed past subsisting beneath the surface of life in capitalist England. Less a 'whole character' than an arena for cultural conflict between past and present, Jude demonstates the irreducible fact that the primitive can only be appropriated if one is well-defended against it.

On the one hand, Jude is the victim of a social process of differentiation and division that erects rigid boundaries to exclude the rural lower classes from the centre of English life. Like Disraeli's Chartists in Sybil, he is both the excluded one and the 'original', with, ironically, a stronger claim to admission to the 'heavenly Jerusalem' – Christminster – than many of the dons. As Raymond Williams notes, Jude is one of the many Hardy stories which enact a 'colonialist' pattern of the 'return of the native', a pattern which dramatizes the inevitable alienation and isolation of one who is both barred from admission to the interior of Christminster and excluded by his education from returning to the life of the rural lower class labourer. As Williams argues,

The ideas, the values, the educated methods are of course made available to us if we get to a place like Christminster: if we are let in as Jude was not. But with the offer, again and again, comes another idea: that the world of everyday work and of ordinary families is inferior, distant; that now we know this world of the mind we can have no respect – and of course no affection – for that other and still familiar world. If we retain an affection, Christminster has a name for it: nostalgia. If we retain respect, Christminster has another name: politics or the even more dreaded 'sociology'.[21]

The ideological barrier of class is, among other things, an educational barrier. Education (metonymically, consciousness) is dual-edged: it fits Jude for living a life from which he is excluded by Christminster, and it unfits him for life in Marygreen. Consequently, in the early part of the book, he spends much of his time acting out a fort/da game of separation and return: walking toward Christminster and then back to Marygreen to the home which is, significantly, not his own home but his aunt's.[22] Moreover, the accessible history of his own family begins, not in Disraelian Romantic unity, but in separation and division, a primal split enacted before conscious memory: although once inhabiting the same house, he and Sue were driven separate ways by the depradations of their parents. And his repetition compulsion drives him forth over roads marked by significant signposts that testify as much to an historical forgetfulness as to memory, roads 'trodden now by he hardly knew whom, though once by many of his own dead family'.[23] The fact that his own family past comes back to him with the shock of the new testifies both to the degree of his deracination and to the visibility of the erasure of that past.

This novel, then, is about obscurity and infamy, forgetfulness and memory; that is, about the pain of the present and the trauma of the past. It is about self-colonization and class-colonization, the exteriorization of a class – the rural artisan class – with an ancient claim of right, and the colonization of two individuals by an alien yet monolithic system of social rules. It is about how a social system of organized domination stamps its own meanings on novel gestures and about how only a Nietzschean refusal to grant final meaning to the historical stream can purchase one a highly tenuous measure of freedom; however, such freedom is bought at a steep price – the price of entrapment in a cycle of eternal recurrence which is the punishment the 'modern' disease of 'self-consciousness' inflicts.

From a diachronic standpoint, *Jude the obscure* distils just the opposite lesson of Disraeli's fiction: to Hardy, knowledge is not power but powerlessness, pain, and suffering. Unlike the Disraelian hero, Hardy's heroes are helpless to press the events of their lives into the service of an expansive ideal or even simply toward a linear historical *telos*. These two opposed perspectives – the synchronic and diachronic – intersect in Hardy's metaphor of landscape. The landscape of Wessex is a privileged place: a symbolic field that is both a stage for the present and a palimpsest of the past, a geographical entity and a collection of signs. To look closely at the land is to find the evolutionary survivals of the past coexisting with the evidence of revolutionary change in the present. Perhaps nowhere is this dual function of the Hardyan landscape better epitomized than in the narrator's description of Stoke-Barehills. Describing this town in Upper Wessex, he says,

The great western highway from London passes through it, near a point where the road branches into two, merely to unite again some twenty miles further westward. Out of this bifurcation and reunion there used to arise among wheeled travellers, before railway days, endless questions of choice between the respective ways. But the question is now as dead as the scot-and-lot free-holder, the road waggoner, and the mail coachman who disputed it; and probably not a single inhabitant of Stoke-Barehills is now even aware that the two roads which part in this town ever meet again; for nobody now drives up and down the great western highway daily. (*Jude*, p. 228)

This description assures a multiple resonance for Stoke-Barehills in this text – psychological, anthropological, and historical. Both a geographical locale, a 'place', as well as a mental configuration whose apparent shape is changed (or lost) by the intrusion of modern civilization in the form of the railroad, it is both a psychological and temporal configuration (the passage describes a separation and subsequent reunion, but a reunion whose origin in separation has been forgotten with the coming of the railroad), and yet, by virtue of that fact, necessarily a figure of highly charged ambivalence.[24] The memory which enables one to 'see' the reunification also forces to consciousness a recollection of painful separation. To forge a unity of the 'whole' in memory is to recall (or to call into existence) the fact of separation. Moreover, the road is a 'survival' of a pre-industrial age, no longer serving any important function. With the lapse of its function, knowledge of its shape has been lost: the implication of this paradox being that the very shape of the 'present' is inaccessible without a knowledge of the past, a knowledge simultaneously precluded by modern civilization's rapid conversion of much of it into non-functional survivals. Memory (and signification) is enabled by loss, as the very positivity of 'survivals' of the past, the consciousness of historical depth, testifies to the fact that the past is now worthless.

Thus, the two roads which surround Stoke-Barehills map the shape of Jude and Sue's plots, the plot of their ancestors, indeed any number of plots in this text. Born of the same family, Sue and Jude are forcibly separated when their parents go different ways, only to begin a dance of reunion in Christminster, after Jude moves there, which culminates in their moving in with each other. Likewise, their 'union' is also a metaphorical 'reunion' of their parents who parted years before the time of the novel. Moreover, this shape is again duplicated in their relationship with their respective 'legal' spouses: both marry early, separate themselves from their mates, and then return to them eventually to lead lives of desperate self-immolation.

The cyclical shapes of these plots suggest something of Hardy's debt to Spencer's *First principles* and his definition of a 'full' history ('An entire history of anything must include its appearance out of the imperceptible and its disappearance into the imperceptible.').[25] The 'life cycle' of human relationships is metaphorically related to the life cycle here, viewed both phylogenetically and ontogenetically: thus, Jude's life begins in orphaned obscurity, skirts the edge of fame (or, more accurately, infamy), and peters out in the obscurity of wasting disease. Yet, as already mentioned, the role of memory is central in the passage on Stoke-Barehills, for the consciousness of oneness is beholden to the memory of separation. To see one's life whole is to be made aware of the painful fact of separateness and division at the same time that one experiences the elation that comes with the growing sense of one's own extension in history. Historical origins shape Jude's present not, as in Disraeli, by predetermining a pattern of reunification as recapitulation of an undivided original state, but by setting an example of primal traumatic division which he must try to avoid but which he is condemned to repeat.[26]

The dialectic of inside and outside which this text foregrounds suggests the 'imperial' themes already examined in this book. Not only does Hardy recognize, as Hillis Miller argues, man's 'dual nature' – both thinking being and willing being – but he analyses the problematic nature of man's dual ontological status – both subject and object at one and the same time – by framing it in terms of 'the unknown country'.[27] Like Disraeli, Kipling, and Carroll, Hardy is obsessed with the Fichtean epistemological dilemma: every attempt to frame the Other leaves a residue which cannot be appropriated – the subject which knows. To know one must be separate from what one knows – one must be cloistered, to an extent, as are the dons of Christminster. Yet the very necessity of this separation suggests that a certain 'unknowability' is intrinsic to the act of knowing: blindness creates the possibility for sight, ignorance for knowledge, unconsciousness for consciousness. The contradiction is obvious but irreducible: to attempt to contain within the sphere of what one knows one's own position as knowing subject is to attempt to contain the unknowable within the field of knowledge.

Like Nietzsche in *Beyond good and evil*, Hardy conjoins both political and psychological themes: the history of the individual enacts the history of the race; both are narratives of conquest and domination, characterized by purely provisional (and ultimately fruitless) attempts to master the 'instinctual' or the 'barbaric' by enclosing it within the circle of knowledge. Jude's ultimate failure to master his own history has wide implications for English history. Like Disraeli's Chartists, Jude is the 'original', exteriorized by the English class system but seeking admission to the interior of English life. In one of his avatars, he represents 'Old England', an England subjected to centuries of conquest by a succession of victorious ruling classes, yet he has also educated himself out of 'Old England' by teaching himself the dead Classical languages. Thus, the novel demonstrates rather neatly the ironic process whereby the highest form of learning which England recognizes is defined as appropriation of the past subject to the absolute condition that one cannot be of the past which one knows: one is modern and civilized insofar as one has an acquaintance with ancient languages but is not oneself 'ancient' (thus, the necessity for excluding Jude from Christminster).

Moreover, while the above definition accords with Matthew Arnold's notion of what it is to be a Classically-educated gentleman, Hardy hints that the past itself, the past which one seeks to 'know', cannot really be effectively appropriated because it is itself riven by contradiction and the tension of opposition: whether it be the incompatible Dionysian and Apollonian faces of Hellenism (Sue distinguishes her 'indecorous' Hellenism from Christminster's 'decorous' variety by repeatedly quoting the subversive Swinburne) or the opposition of the subjugated Celtic 'Old England' and its maypole to the Roman conquerors. Jude's position is perfectly anomalous in that he is a representative of the English past by virtue of his class position and an educated man who 'knows' in ways that Christminster ought to recognize as its own way of 'knowing'. By excluding him, Christminster condemns him to a limbo between cultures while ratifying its own ignorance as knowledge.

Needless to say, this implies that Hardy's notion of history is, not surprisingly, multiply ambiguous. To Hardy history is both a selection of the remarkable, the novel occurrences of the past, as well as the fact of repetition, the endlessly repeated cycle of the same – generation, growth, death, and birth. Hardy's 'history' is traced by the irreconcilably contradictory meanings we have already suggested: change and continuity, fissure and connection, destruction and creation, difference and sameness. Appropriately, Hardy is as interested in the forgetting of history as he is in the reading of historical survivals, for the perpetual forgetting of history is one of the most incorrigible of historical 'facts'. As his description of spring ploughing reveals, farming itself – that consummately 'pre-industrial' form of economic activity – is an activity which constantly works to obliterate the traces of the past; in a newly-ploughed field, history is only accessible under the sign of erasure, as an inference one makes in the face of the evidence of its obliteration.[28] Hardy both laments the passing of the old ways and the historical marginalization of an atavistic social class, and yet constructs a novel in which fundamental change is shown to be ultimately illusory.

Thus, Jude's story begins as if it were going to unfold as a conventional Victorian *Bildungsroman*: his interest in getting to Christminster feeds his interest in acquiring the necessary skills – Classical languages. In 'improving himself', he not only moves closer, so he thinks, to attaining his goal of admission to Christminster, but each return to Marygreen is but a momentary delay and deferral of his mission which deepens his historical consciousness, his sense of extension into the past, by reminding him of past trauma which he must surmount. Early in the book he casts himself as Bunyan's Christian on his way to the 'heavenly Jerusalem'. His returns to Marygreen here, like Tancred's recapitulations of originary relationships, merely sanctify a belief in the necessity of ultimate progress, for 'progress', in this literary form, is always a 'return' to something more ancient. Thus, after seeing (or imagining) Christminster from the ladder, he runs home, fortified with the comfort that his aunt's cottage affords, 'even though this was not the home of his birth, and his great-aunt did not care much about him' (*Jude*, p. 19) – a Hardyan rendering of Jude's ultimate alienation both from Christminster and Marygreen, the forbidding fortress of his aspiration and the modest cottage of his birth.

His renewal of hope in being accepted at Christminster, which commences soon after he breaks up with Arabella, places him in the same unstable position as Clym Yeobright facing his imminent blindness in *The return of the native*:

For a moment there fell on Jude a true illumination; that here in the stone yard was a centre of effort as worthy as that dignified by the name of scholarly study within the noblest of the colleges. But he lost it under the stress of his old idea. He would accept any employment which might be offered him on the strength of his late employer's recommendation; but he would accept it as a provisional thing only . This was his form of the modern vice of unrest. (*Jude*, p. 68)

The momentary belief that the two spheres are equal gives way under the pressure of an 'old idea': that the life of the mind which commences in the interior of Christminster's buildings is superior to the life of the medieval artisan working on the exterior of those same buildings. Exclusion is the spur to desire, especially if that from which one is excluded is 'old', an 'ancient' desire. Thus, the incest theme which haunts Jude's relationship with Sue is equated with the political theme of his exclusion from Christminster. Exclusion or interdiction spurs desire while frustrating fulfilment; historical precedence determines affective intensity.

Thus, this entire Christminster passage is marked by Jude's restlessly fluctuating between accepting his exclusion from Christminster by consoling himself with the realization that those who work on the 'exterior' are essential to the work of the place, a kind of material substratum which enables the 'ideal' work of the college. ('He saw that his destiny lay not with these, but among the manual toilers in the shabby purlieu which he himself occupied, unrecognized as part of the city at all by its visitors and panegyrists, yet without whose denizens the hard readers could not read nor the high thinkers live', *Jude*, p. 94.) While this realization might make "obscurity" bearable, as the price one must pay for the profound pleasure of feeling oneself to be foundational, the Tory in Hardy also acknowledges here that the fact of exclusion – the barrier itself – is what articulates value: the value of the life of the mind behind Christminster's walls and of the work of the artisans who labour on its exterior. The 'coming universal wish' to surmount these barriers threatens the value of both kinds of work by threatening the defining distinction between the two.

This paradox plays itself out in this novel in many forms, among others, in Hardy's attempt to place man as subject/object within nature: as Beer argues, to contain the history of consciousness within a longer, all-encompassing history which extends before and beyond the horizon of consciousness.[29] Yet Jude's arrival in Christminster affords Hardy the opportunity to hint at the blindness of Christminster as well. And, because of the complex transferential structure of this novel, we must see Jude's own failure to read and master his past in order to avoid replaying it as setting the pattern for Christminster's own exclusion of him from its walls. Jude's plot, in other words, is Christminster's plot: Jude is at once the *pharmakos* expelled from the holy city of Christminster – the highest as well as the lowest embodiment of its civilization and, like Oedipus of Thebes, condemned to exile as a result – and Christminster itself, expelling his own unknowable *pharmakoi* – his past, his sexuality – in a purification rite which establishes himself at the cost of dividing himself. Thus, Christminster's expulsion of the Dionysian face of Hellenism, its valorization of an Arnoldian "Great Books" Classicism and consequent devaluation (really ignorance) of the creative/destructive Hellenism celebrated by Swinburne, Pater, and Nietzsche among Hardy's contemporaries,[30] sets a pattern which Jude will repeat in his own plot, although he remains permanently attracted to the person who embodies, early on, precisely what Christminster censors – the 'Swinburnean' Sue of the first half of the novel.

Thus, Jude arrives at Christminster early in the book as a representative of the past, a past which the students and dons do not recognize:

Although people moved round him he virtually saw none. Not as yet having mingled with the active life of the place it was largely non-existent to him. But the saints and prophets in the windows-tracery, the paintings in the galleries, the statues, the busts, the gargoyles, the corbel-heads – these seemed to breathe his atmosphere. Like all newcomers to a spot on which the past is deeply graven he heard that past announcing itself with an emphasis altogether unsuspected by, and even incredible to, the habitual residents. (Jude, p. 69)

The privilege of the outside is the privilege of a particular form of consciousness: Jude 'sees' the past but not the present of Christminster; he is free of the tyranny of habit which blinds the students and dons.

Yet Jude's impulse, at this point, is to overcome the alienating distance between himself and those 'happy young contemporaries of his with whom he shared a common mental life', to leap the formidable 'wall' which divides him from them in a utopian gesture of pure identification oblivious to the barrier of class:

Yet he was as far from them as if he had been at the antipodes. Of course he was. He was a young workman in a white blouse, and with stone-dust in the creases of his clothes; and in passing him they did not even see him, or hear him, rather saw through him as through a pane of glass at their familiars beyond. Whatever they were to him, he to them was not on the spot at all; and yet he had fancied he would be close to their lives by coming there. (Jude, pp. 69-70)

It is significant here that Jude, who can see Christminster's past (or, at least, is ever aware that it has a past, however problematic its accessibility), cannot be seen by the students at the University. In fact, Hardy constructs a self-referential abyss here at the edge of which Jude teeters. That the students do not see Jude suggests that they do not see the past, or, at least, that part of the past which Jude represents: that is the blindness which constitutes their sight. Moreover, they only see their 'familiars', reinforcing the suggestion that their knowledge is notably self-referential. Yet, insofar as Jude identifies with them, he sees what they see: that is, he also does not see himself. Thus, it is significant that in the act of imbibing the 'Christminster sentiment', he is 'surprised by impish echoes of his own footsteps, smart as the blows of a mallet' [Jude, p. 69]: a rendering of traces of his subjectivity appropriated only in their alienation. Moreover, this passage also parallels Sue's sympathetic identification with Jude's feelings at the time of her marriage to Phillotson, a parallel reinforcing the complex transferential relationship between Christminster, Jude, and Sue.

When Jude receives his disillusioning letter from the Master of Biblioll to whom he had applied for help in entering the University, he proceeds to get drunk and then descends to Crossway to meditate on the historical significance of this juncture:

It had more history than the oldest college in the city. It was literally teeming, stratified, with the shades of human groups, who had met there for tragedy, comedy, farce; real enactments of the intensest kind. At Fourways men had stood and talked of Napoleon, the loss of America, the execution of King Charles, the burning of the Martyrs, the Crusades, the Norman Conquest, possibly of the arrival of Caesar. Here the two sexes had met for loving, hating, coupling, parting; had waited, had suffered, for each other; had triumphed over each other; cursed each other in jealousy, blessed each other in forgiveness. (*Jude*, p. 95)

More than simply Jude's assertion of the more ancient claims of his class of common people to the centre of English life in the face of of Christminster's rebuff, a personal deconstruction of the social hierarchy of Christminster ('He began to see that the town life was a book of humanity infinitely more palpitating, varied, and compendious than the gown life', *Jude*, p. 95), this passage introduces the evolutionary geological metaphor ('stratified') which conditions Hardy's notion of history.[31] History in this novel presents itself as a chasm: all of the past would be simultaneously available to consciousness if one could only read its signs, decipher the meaning of the various layers of rock which support the ground on which men walk in the present. However, this does not at all guarantee its presence to consciousness, in part because history is also the history of the repression or erasure of history.[32] Moreover, to extend the metaphor, the past is the foundation of the present, as the lower geological layers physically support the upper. In other words, to follow out these implications, Christminster does not 'know itself' because it does not know what it is not: if what it has surmounted or overcome or forgotten is its foundation, then its knowledge is constituted by a willed ignorance of what is most fundamental. Hardy does not innocently balance two separate but equal spheres here, but rather, deconstructs the 'town/gown' opposition by displacing it in a geological metaphor which inverts the conventional hierarchy, meanwhile insinuating also that Jude's own 'present' rests on a parallel 'forgetting' or repression of his own foundation, his own past.

Thus, the present (or Christminster) arrogates to itself, wrongly in Jude's view, the privilege of hierarchical ascendancy: it is the top layer of a stratified system. To assert, then, as Jude does, the claims of the 'foundation' against the arrogant smugness of the superstructure is to remind the Christminster dons of their debt to anonymous medieval workmen, to remind the present that it rests on a past which still has claims of right, to remind the metropolis of its debt to the periphery. Moreover, to locate, as Hardy does, Jude and the workmen in Christminster is to suggest that the past, the uncivilized, the unknowable is somehow immanent in the present, the civilized, the knowers; that each of these define themselves in opposition to one another through an act of exclusion which is really an act of self-division. The tragic *pharmakos* which must be expelled from Christminster's view to constitute Christminster's 'knowledge' must be one of Christminster's own thrust out from within. However, to be conscious of that past is to place oneself outside it in order to know it: hence, Jude's ironic status among the working class of Christminster – he is the one who 'knows' the 'other' past in a way that Christminster's dons would have to acknowledge is an acceptable way of 'knowing', and he is, finally, the victim in a primeval sacrifical ritual conducted on Remembrance Day in Mr. Donn's pork shop.[33]

Moreover, in Hardy the 'crossroads' is the privileged site for the irruption of the past into the present. Like the crossroads in *Oedipus rex* which carries a multiple signification – as the site of the parricide, it is the place where Oedipus performs the destructive act which makes his mother a widow and thus leaves her available to him as a sexual partner, a signifier of the intersection of past and present, destruction and creation – 'Crossway' suggests the coupling of creation and destruction, life and death, the organic and the inorganic, that structure the contradictory nature of plot or destiny.

Jude's exclusion from the intellectual life of Christminster then follows rather quickly an earlier exclusion with which it is paralleled: from marriage with Sue Bridehead. Jude is both Sue's opposite – the one who helps define her individuality by opposing her – and a part of her. Thus, in making both Sue and Jude members of the same family, in fact, consistently underlining their identity and then constructing a courtship for them, Hardy re-enacts the same tragic sequence of self-division of a unitary whole, expulsion of the *pharmakos*, and fruitless attempts at reunification which follow that expulsion. Moreover, Jude reads Sue's acceptance of Phillotson's offer of marriage as a reproach to himself. ('Her reproach had taken that shape, then, and not the shape of words', *Jude*, p. 107.) By marrying Phillotson, Sue deliberately interdicts herself from Jude while simultaneously establishing an intimate distance between herself and him. She calls upon their ties of kinship in asking Jude to rehearse her wedding with Phillotson and then to give her away: first, as already mentioned, with Jude 'playing' her husband, then, during the legal ceremony, with Jude playing her father (*Jude*, p. 137). The combinations of distance and intimacy which these charades produce not only feed Jude's desire for her,[34] but they do so by drawing his attention, again and again, to the unpleasant fact that he is up against a wall as formidable as any in Christminster. To force him to play her father at her wedding is to raise the stakes in their flirtation by suggesting (by tortuous artifice) the enticing and forbidden possibility of an incestuous liaison. More importantly, Sue's Hellenism, her infatuation with 'Greek joyousness', erects a barrier between them which it becomes Jude's intention to surmount, a task which he accomplishes only temporarily and symbolically in his room when he dresses the 'wet Greek deity' in his own clothes. By the time Jude is fully ready to embrace the goal of 'Greek joyousness', Sue has gone far in the opposite direction, practising a forbidding, Christian pietistic self-flagellation.

When they move in together, Sue insists to Phillotson that her living with Jude signifies just the opposite of love (a sign both of her own naïveté and of the cyclical repetitiveness of Jude's plot): in one sense, this can be seen as Jude's return to the home of his infancy when Sue lived in the same house. Yet, after their first passionate kiss following the death of Aunt Drusilla, they begin the long process of switching places with each other: Sue embarking on the road to becoming an apostle of virtuous renunciation and Jude gradually heading towards becoming the spokesman for 'Greek joyousness' and instinctual liberation. Thus, he gives up his Christminster scheme again at this point, holding that he is no longer fit to observe the moral standards of the role, and burns his theological books: a gesture which, like so many in this novel, reaffirms in ritual fashion the legitimacy of the social rules he would repudiate (Jude, pp. 171-2). In symbolic terms, both Jude and Sue are approaching the condition of family members, bound by ties of sublimated sexual passion, yet unable to take any real comfort in this relationship because of its tortuous ambiguity. The novel persistently implies that they are family members *and* lovers, as it persistently asserts that Jude is in Christminster *and* that he is not, as it asserts that the past is the present *and* that it is not, as it asserts that creation is destruction *and* that it is not.

In this respect, the two lovers come to stand metonymically for the process of definition by alienation which we have been discussing in this book. Children of the same home and first cousins by birth, they are eventually even identified by Phillotson as two halves of one split person. (See Phillotson: 'They seem to be one person split in two!' *Jude*, p. 182.) In fact, Sue's own father was a medieval artisan like Jude (*Jude*, p. 80). Moreover, Jude plays the role of tragic scapegoat in his relation with Sue and Phillotson early in the book. In a passage which parallels the one in which he observes the Christminster students while remaining himself unobserved, he watches Phillotson place his arm around a reluctant Sue while she looks around but not far enough around to observe Jude sinking into 'the hedge like one struck with a blight' (*Jude*, p. 88). Moreover, Sue's perpetual virginity (cf. 'I have remained as I began', *Jude*, p. 118) suggests not only her own frigidity and sterility but, by virtue of the identification Hardy establishes between the two 'lovers', casts light on Jude's cyclical plot as well: life lived as a series of recapitulations implies a perpetual virginity in both positive and negative senses – perpetual sterility and naïveté as well as perpetually renewed openness to new experience, to new plot. Thus, Jude's response to Arabella, newly returned from Australia, suggests both his own inability to master his past, to place himself outside the plots of the past, as well as an admirable self-consistency in the form of his desires: 'I am as I was' (*Jude*, p. 144).

The cyclical structure and the predominance of mirroring desires here suggests that Hardy offers no simple key to unlocking the complex transferential relationships in this book. The 'origin' of desire is lost in a play of mirrors, just as the authority of the past over the present is asserted beyond consciousness. The key to Sue's enigmatic motives should be found in Jude, but such an observation merely begs the question of what those might be for while her 'desires' are introjected versions of his, his also come to mirror hers (as Jude's more 'ancient' desire to breach the wall of Christminster mirrors his mentor Phillotson's, Sue's initial frigidity mirrors Jude's own Christian chastity from the time when they first met). Jude's expressions are often governed by his need to do what is best by Sue – even if that requires, contradictorily, renouncing her. Likewise, as we have already demonstrated, Jude recapitulates in his own plot the complex and ultimately fruitless process of self-definition and self-integration by expulsion of the *pharmakos* which characterizes Christminster's relationship with him. These endless cycles of recapitulation without a point of origination are the most interesting expressions in this book of the play of eternal recurrence which governs Hardy's notion of history.

The interplay of innocence and experience, forgetfulness and memory, bespeaks an ignorance which can somehow be renewed even after it has been dispelled: plot is not a linear movement from ignorance to knowledge but a cyclical repetition of an ignorance which looks like knowledge and knowledge which looks like ignorance. Ultimately, the model for what Hardy is attempting to accomplish is something like Nietzsche's doctrine of 'eternal recurrence', a model which Hardy undoubtedly would have refused to acknowledge, bound as he seems to have been to the popular English view of Nietzsche at the turn of the century.[35] Nevertheless, the paradox of history – the fact of change and difference coexisting with continuity and repetition, or rather, change and difference as alternative ways of conceptualizing continuity and repetition – which Hardy seems intent to work out in the pages of his book shares many similarities to Nietzsche's conception, and the intellectual influences to which Hardy subjected himself at the end of the nineteenth century (Schopenhauer, Weismann's *Essays upon heredity*, Spencer's *First principles*) suggest he could have been moving in a Nietzschean direction at the time he wrote *Jude*.

In the notes which were collected together posthumously and issued as *The will to power*, Nietzsche defines the eternal recurrence as, in a sense, a necessary postulate to a philosophy which eschews ultimate ends while emphasizing will-to-power: 'existence as it is, without meaning or aim, yet recurring inevitably without any finale of nothingness'.[36] As I have demonstrated, Hardy's vision of history, like Nietzsche's, is anti-teleological: Jude's only ultimate 'end' in life is death or release from the tragic repetitiveness of existence. Like Freud's claim in *Beyond the pleasure principle* ('The aim of all life is death'), such an 'end' is an anti-teleological refusal of meaning to the stream of life which, for instance, religious *teloi* promise: death as return to the inorganic, a release from the burden of desire – pure quiescence. Spencer's notion of vital process as one of emergence out of obscurity and homogeneity and into differentiation and heterogeneity, followed by a return to obscurity is obviously an important influence here, although, like Freud's, it is cast in inescapably teleological form.

Moreover, Nietzsche offers the hypothesis of the eternal recurrence as a way of accounting for the portents of meaning which the recurrences of life seem to signal, while denying the promise of ultimate mastery of the meaning of one's life (or of history) that is promised by arrival at the 'end' of existence. Thus, as Nietzsche argues, 'To impose upon becoming the character of being – that is the supreme will-to-power' (p. 330). The will-to-power thus calls into existence an eschatology which, ironically, refuses to perform the function all good eschatologies should: the eternal recurrence guarantees that repetition necessary to generate the portents of meaning (metaphor, for instance, is obviously beholden to the sense of repetition) while denying the necessary point of closure to history – for such 'ends' infinitely repeat themselves endlessly. It implies endless repetition, endless sameness, while conceptualizing that repetition as a series of historical events – differences – which are repeated point for point.

Moreover, Nietzsche offers this doctrine as a means of reconciling ethical choice and determinism: the thought that what one does in life – the shame one brings on oneself by one's vile actions, the credit which accrues from good acts – will be repeated point for point for eternity ought to operate as a powerful inspiration to 'noble' behaviour. Yet the obvious determinism of this scheme ought to undermine such a possibility ('change' or 'improvement', moral or otherwise, would obviously destroy the symmetry of the repetition), although it is also consonant with a tragic notion of the fateful coherence of the individual life: whatever one has done (whether noble or ignoble) is an appropriate, a meaningful expression of one's character; one could not have done otherwise. One finally must say with Jude, 'I am as I was'.

Thus, the 'bleak' ending of Jude the obscure – Sue returned to Phillotson, Jude to Arabella and a slow wasting death – closes the cycle of their plot-lives by returning them to an earlier point in their own histories. Yet the narrative implies both that Jude's death is a recapitulation of his birth, a return to a time before death, and something different – a sacrifice which parallels Sue's sacrifice of her body to the loathsome Phillotson. As he was once the reluctant butcher, Jude is now the pig, the victim, his life slowly ebbing away in Donn's pork shop, his sacrifice at the hands of Arabella merely the last repetition of a life of sacrifice. Yet the cosmic justice of this final scene is underlined in the fact that it is a replaying of an earlier sacrifice but with the chief roles reversed: the butcher become the victim. His failure to realize his dream of becoming a don, like his failure to marry Sue, suggests both that his own personal existence is governed by an imperative of eternal return – an ontological stasis which is the cultural counterpart of the cosmic cyclical stasis (birth, growth, decay, and death) to which all organic life is subject – and that the failure of this member of an atavistic social class to 'rise' serves the ideological interests of the institution which defines the civilized – Christminster – and which requires the persistence of the primitive outside its gates but inside England.

As an arena for cultural conflict between civilization and the primitive past, Jude's self-division is the measure of the degree of his deracination. Moreover, deracination of this sort still ensures one an important social role: in Jude's case, the perpetual victim-scapegoat whose exteriorization ensures the integrity, the solidity, of the barriers which articulate a cultural space in which the civilized opposes the primitive. Jude's anomalous status ensures the existence of the walls – psychological, intellectual, and class – which ensure Christminster's social role as the apogee of English civilization. In a sense, all three of the novels we have been discussing take the prominent Victorian theme of inheritance and transmute it: on the one hand, Haggard's heroes, while they ultimately act in the interests of repression, celebrate the fitness of their relationship, their affiliation, with the ancient civilization of Kôr; Conrad and Hardy, on the other hand, question the culturally-imposed boundaries between past and present, primitive and civilized: the distinction between the two they find to be both historically arbitrary and ethically imperative. Where Marlow ultimately comes around to celebrating all articulation of the darkness as a kind of necessary idolatry, Conrad deliberately dissolves the differences to locate their foundation purely in the self-serving mythology of the conqueror. Marlow gloats over his role in disabusing his listeners of their own ethnocentrically moralistic prejudices, but his amoralism finally commits him to the celebration of empire for its own sake: the man who gives us Kurtz is also Kurtz's apologist in the end. Hardy, like Conrad, collapses the cultural distinction between the primitive and the civilized by underlining their uncanny recapitulation of each other – English 'civilization' performs a 'primitive' scapegoating ritual with Jude – but his vision of the life of the individual as an arena for cultural, psychological, and physical conflict between opposing forces reasserts the necessity – cultural and 'natural' – of the barriers Jude challenges.

IV

With this consideration of *Jude the obscure* we have come full circle in this book. The class issues raised by *Jude* recall the atmosphere of Disraeli's social novels *Coningsby* and *Sybil*. As we have demonstrated, the structure of class relationships within England is conceived by Disraeli along lines that are best described as imperial. Not only does Disraelian conservatism require the existence of an outside threat and the opportunity it offers to deflect attention from the reality of what it acknowledges are probably irresolvable domestic class conflicts, but Disraeli's upper-class heroes are able to bring the lower and middle-classes into their 'proper' inheritance of political power only on the condition that these classes submit to what is best described as a process of 'colonization' and domestication. Thus, Dandy Mick in Sybil is allowed a place in the new social synthesis that follows the suppression of 'Bishop' Hatton's riot only on the condition that he submit to being tamed by Egremont. In Disraeli, the legitimacy of aristocratic rule is reinforced by the maintenance of the lower orders in a state of dependency that is rationalized, not so much by the ideology of inequality of blood, but rather by the need to effect rapid social change while preserving the 'natural' aristocratic structure of English society.

Moreover, the central importance of the idea of empire to the kind of hierarchical society Disraeli sought to maintain is revealed baldly in Tancred. Empire, in Disraeli's view, fashions gentlemen of substance out of erstwhile parochial, bored aristocrats, thus providing a small measure of justification for the social and political privileges of a class which expends wealth but does not, in nineteenth-century eyes, seem to produce much of it. Tancred employs recognizably 'middle-class' character traits – renunciation of immediate gratification, devotion to 'duty' – in the service of 'higher' goals than the purely material ones Disraeli associates with the objects of middle-class striving. However, these 'higher goals' ultimately amount to a kind of 'motiveless' playing at empire which finally threatens, in subterranean fashion, the cultural hierarchies it is meant to shore up.

As Chapter 2 demonstrates, this construction of empire as 'playing field' is developed at greater length in the works of Burton and Kipling, both of whom employ the metaphor of culture as 'game' to take advantage of the metaphor's critical power. To identify a cultural event as a game is to subject it to a process of questioning which eliminates its metaphysical sanction: games are consummately human, not divine, creations. To be able to play many games, to embrace the constant shifting of cultural identities, is to rise above, to an extent, the boorish ethnocentrism which distorts the perceptions of most of the Europeans who live in the Middle East or India. For most European notions of superiority are grounded in a form of essentialism: the belief that there is a European (or English) essence – whether biological, cultural, racial, or intellectual – which sets Europeans apart from – and therefore above, in a substantial way – alien peoples. That

Burton and Kipling use this novel stance as the basis for a critique of British ethnocentrism testifies to the corrosive power of the conception. That both also try to arrest that critique at critical points in order to hold onto more traditional beliefs – whether it is Burton's rather banal need to believe that Egyptians are capable of discipline but not of higher thought processes or Kipling's more sophisticated belief in Britain's political mission to order the world – testifies to a common Victorian anxiety about maintaining certain crucial guideposts – even if they have already been discredited – in a world in which the critique of ethnocentrism opens up the insupportable prospect of a flattening of all cultural values.

In a sense, Carroll's Alice finds herself immersed in just such a nightmare in Wonderland. As the most impressive literary critique of the epistemological grounds of cultural imperialism in the nineteenth century, *Alice* demonstrates the complicity between ethnocentrism and the very notion of 'value'. Alice's failure to appropriate successfully the 'creatures' in Wonderland, and her inability to force fit those she cannot understand into her own ethnocentric categories, plunges her into a nightmare world that comes to reflect, in an uncanny way, her own narrowness. The values she has inherited are relatively useless to her for they merely serve to emphasize her distance from the creatures she seeks to comprehend, yet, trapped in a world populated by beings who subscribe to customs fundamentally different from her own, she relies even more heavily on these values that serve her so ill. Carroll's critique of the imperial child is an oblique attack on the necessary alliance between a narrow culture and the values it seeks to instil in its young. If Tancred's 'Grand Tour' is a broadening experience, Alice's is a narrowing one, for her confrontation with the alien freezes her into her rigid set of ethnocentric prejudices which offer her no hope of mastering her environment. *Wonderland* is an 'Anti-Bildungsroman' in which the failure to achieve adulthood is a direct consequence of the attempt to play the imperialist: an indirect repudiation of Disraeli's myth of imperial adventure as the road to true maturity.

The late century 'crisis of the civilized', which was inspired partly through the accelerating pace of accumulation of anthropological 'knowledge' of 'primitive' ways of life (itself a consequence of Europe's world-wide political hegemony) and partly through Darwinism's influential emphasis on mankind's affiliation with the animal world, also arises as a consequence of a new cultural 'humility' which comes of attempting to cast the ontogenetic question we have been discussing in phylogenetic terms: not so much 'How does the child become the imperial adult?' but 'How did savagery give rise to civilization?' While the doctrine of 'survivals' represents a psychological defence against the full implications of the newly established kinship between the civilized and the savage, it was also instrumental in inspiring the literary treatments of the relationship between savage and civilized that we have discussed here, treatments which challenge the conventional difference. While Haggard's novels treat the savage past as a box to be opened and then firmly closed again to keep it from contaminating the civilized present, Conrad's Marlow opens the box only to discover that Pandora has been there before him – that the civilized is always already contaminated by a savagery it thinks it is containing by conquest.

With Hardy's *Jude*, the interplay of distance and filiation between civilized present and the 'savage' past which is also its origin is cast as the quintessential form of a cultural ambivalence which structures all aspects of life: the relationship of male to female, consciousness to unconsciousness, modern industrial England to an atavistic social class. With Jude's failure to 'develop', Hardy sounds the death knell to the kind of imperial optimism which grounded Disraeli's hopes for an England which would 'grow' by incorporating the remade alien. If Hardy is a 'pessimist', it is because he sees the Victorian cultural technology of 'domestication' as grounded in a primitive scapegoating ritual which is both ethically insupportable and culturally inescapable.

Disposing of the surplus:
capitalism and empire

With the heating up of European imperial rivalries in the latter part of the nineteenth century, the question of why nations engage in imperial expansion inevitably comes to the fore. Moreover, an adequate answer to this question would have to take account of the fact that the European powers competing for *Lebensraum* at this time are, with the exception of Czarist Russia, developed capitalist societies. In an earlier age, when Britain stood alone with the most highly developed capitalist economy, the question of whether industrialism carries with it an inherent tendency to overseas expansion was not usually part of the debate. The Cobdenites, for example, were the most prominent theorists of the connection between industry and empire in the early-Victorian age, and they argued that empire was economically useless, indeed, damaging to the home country's economic health.[1]

The most prominent mid-Victorian attempts to vindicate Britain's imperial mission (Dilke's *Greater Britain*, Froude's *Oceana*, and Seeley's *The expansion of England*) all acknowledge, in contrast to the Cobdenite position, that Britain's colonies have made Britain richer than she would otherwise have been, but nevertheless search beyond economics for reasons why Britain should continue its 'mission'.[2] Victorian social reformers and radicals like Charles Dilke promoted English nationalism because they wanted colonies available to absorb the unemployed without sacrificing the 'radical' political influence of these 'sons' (Arendt, p. 181). And Seeley's now-notorious claim 'We seem, as it were, to have conquered and people half the world in a fit of absence of mind' (Seeley, p. 8) is the opening wedge for his argument for England's acknowledging its 'world-historical mission'. For Seeley, the 'cause' of Britain's 'expansion' must be sought, not in the attractions of wealth which, he acknowledges, colonies do offer their possessors, but in the 'great idea' of expansion itself: the 'expansion of England' is, he claims, the 'telos' that makes Britain's history, and especially the history of its eighteenth-century wars with France for India and the New World, meaningful (Seeley, p. 36). Through an Hegelian act of retrospective reading, Seeley seeks to make England conscious of the meaning of what it has always been doing so that it will go about its future imperial business forthrightly and rationally.

The Idealist tone of this 'vindication' of empire, however, has a limited appeal in the disenchanted atmosphere of the period from the Jameson Raid to the end of the last Boer War. The widespread belief that Cecil Rhodes and his fellow financiers had manipulated Britain into an unwanted and costly war against the South African Boers would, when the full cost of that venture in English lives was computed, feed the growing suspicion that late nineteenth-century finance capital – not some evanescent 'spirit of expansion'—was somehow implicated in the dirty game of imperial adventure.[3] In addition, the neo-mercantilist argument that Britain might make economically profitable use of its relationship to its colonies by establishing trading monopolies with them would be revived and popularized by Joseph Chamberlain in the 'imperial federation' scheme on which he staked his political career at the turn of the century. Although his scheme was not as popular as he had hoped, his modest political success testifies to a growing interest at this time in the connection between capitalism and empire.[4]

The publication in 1902 of J. A. Hobson's *Imperialism: a study* is an important event in the contest of ideologies for, in that book for the first time, British imperial appetites are analysed from the standpoint of an economy of the supplement. More than simply an economic argument, although it is for its economic argument – the so-called 'underconsumptionist' argument – that this book has achieved its greatest notoriety, Hobson's *Imperialism* seeks to demonstrate that empire serves to absorb the dangerous overflow of British culture in all respects – both surplus population and surplus capital. In the process, rather than simply restating a familiar late nineteenth-century 'frontier' thesis of the sort employed by Dilke, Hobson asserts that this process of exporting capital and surplus population is necessary to late capitalism – what was coming to be called 'monopoly capitalism'— because it allows Britain to achieve social equilibrium without the necessity of a revolutionary reshaping of its society and relations of production. To Hobson, in effect, mature capitalist societies need colonies because they absorb workers and capital whose employment at home would otherwise require a radical redistribution of wealth – a revolution, in short.

To Hobson, Britain's excess – whether people or capital – is not innocent, for it actually threatens the foundation of a society built on inequality and privilege. This 'dangerous supplement' must be 'invested' safely overseas. Although seemingly exterior to Britain's economic system, the colonies are rather essential to it, essential by virtue of constituting a field for the deployment of the home country's otherwise destabilizing surplus. This investment of the surplus on the margins of its economic sphere is precisely what enables the system to function as well as it does at home.

The 'sociological' argument of the book addresses an issue that had already an ancient lineage by the time Hobson came to it, indeed, early political economy having already constituted itself by addressing the twin issues of surplus population and surplus labour. Malthus's name is, of course, associated with the view that overbreeding among the poorer classes would lead population growth, eventually, to outstrip increases in the food supply. And Ricardo's faith that a vast increase in the number of workers would eventually, through the inexorable laws of supply and demand, drive wages down to subsistence level was to be endorsed by Marx as an inevitable outcome of the current operation of the capitalist system. Moreover, one of Britain's colonies had already been used as a dumping ground for Britain's surplus criminal population in the late eighteenth and early nineteenth century, and Australia's crucial role in bleeding off these marginal members of British society was often applauded as a guarantee of the health of Britain's body politic.[5] Thus, in casting the colonies in the role of employment agency for those who are unemployable at home, Hobson is simply reformulating a commonplace of Victorian social criticism:

In all the professions, military and civil, the army, diplomacy, Church, the bar, teaching and engineering, Greater Britain serves for an overflow, relieving the congestion of the home market and offering chances to more reckless or adventurous members, while it furnishes a convenient limbo for damaged characters and careers.[6]

However, in identifying specifically 'modern' imperialism, that is, imperialism which serves the interests of an investing class with formidable assets, Hobson makes a unique contribution. While he pays lip service in a late preface to the argument, advanced by contemporary social Darwinists like Karl Pearson, that the motive for imperialism is 'rooted in some ineradicable pugnacity and predacity of the animal man' (Hobson, p. xii), he finds such naturalistic explanations ultimately very unsatisfying. More compelling is the idea that 'modern' imperialism is driven by motives that are economic in origin, but serve the interests of a small group of wealthy, politically influential investors, sometimes to the detriment of the economic self-interest of Britain as a whole. His claim that 'the modern foreign policy of Great Britain has been primarily a struggle for profitable markets for investment' (Hobson, p. 53) is made with Joseph Chamberlain's 'imperial federation' scheme in mind but with one major difference: where Chamberlain offers his scheme under the politically 'innocent' guise of a novel way of using Britain's overseas empire, Hobson reads recent British expansionism as always already driven by the motive of profit, particularly private profit.[7] Chamberlain's imperial federation would, if put into practice, merely formalize (and stultify) a relationship currently flourishing without the rigidity of protective tariffs.

Hobson's diagnosis of the ills of imperial expansionism – its tendency to stifle the zeal for redistributive policies at home which ultimately hold out the only hope for the British industrial surplus realizing an improvement in the lot of the vast majority of Britons – had an important influence on the twentieth-century polemics of capitalism and empire. Among Marxists, Hobson's ideas were recirculated and reinterpreted, first by Hilferding in his Monopoly capital (1910) and later in the works of Lenin (Imperialism, the highest stage of capitalism, 1917) and Rosa Luxemburg (The accumulation of capital, 1918).[8] Relying heavily on the main features of Hobson's argument but dismissing as idle bourgeois optimism Hobson's hope that monopoly capital's tendency to overseas expansion could be curtailed by policies which stoked internal demand and redistributed wealth from the rentier class to the working class, Lenin sees imperialism as the culminating stage of capitalism – the historical telos toward which capitalism was moving from its inception, and the end which will pre-cipitate the inevitable destruction of the capitalist state (Lenin, pp. 266-302). Written in the midst of the Great War, a conflict seen by many European intellectuals as the inevitable outgrowth of intensify-ing imperial rivalries among the great powers during the latter part of the nineteenth century, its strident tone clearly shaped by the ideological imperatives under which he himself operated during 1916, Lenin's essay nevertheless stated a position with some attraction for European intellectuals during the war. So widespread was the belief

that capitalism's 'monopoly' stage was responsible both for the
policies of imperial expansion and for the destructive world war
which imperial rivalry seemed to have spawned that in the immediate
post-war period it could be said to have attained the status of left-wing
orthodoxy.

The challenge to this orthodoxy was not long in coming, however.
Perhaps the most effective challenge was made by an Austrian
sociologist, a student of Max Weber's, who later achieved fame in an
American academic career which brought him to Harvard during the
1930s. Joseph Schumpeter's essay 'The sociology of imperialism' was
published in 1919, and it offers a very interesting and, in some
respects, compelling, although ultimately unsatisfying historical
examination of the connection between empire and capitalism, an
explanation which traces the causes of imperialism, not to economic,
but to sociological and psychological roots.[9] Moreover, the general
conclusion which Schumpeter draws – that the impetus for modern
imperial policies is to be found, not in the inherent tendencies of
monopoly capitalism, but in the political influence of pre-capitalist
aristo-military castes in Europe – seeks ultimately to absolve capitalism
of responsibility for modern European imperialism. Yet that general
conclusion is symptomatically grounded in a logic which classifies
imperial 'attitudes' as 'survivals': a deployment which ultimately
renders problematic his attempt to explain their political efficacy. The
'supplementary' logic which governs his discourse finally swallows up
any chance he will explain imperialism, leaving him bound to consign
imperial 'attitudes' to the realm of useless atavisms, but atavisms
which, somehow, have largely determined modern history.

Schumpeter relies on a notion of 'rationality' inherited from
political economy. Like his mentor Weber, he sees modern history in
the capitalist West as shaped by a gradual process of 'rationalization'
of all aspects of social experience: production, consumption, work,
play, and so on. The history of modern capitalist societies is a story
of the gradual absorption of populations into the market economy and
the training of them in the ethos of capitalism. Crucial to this notion
of 'rationality' is the belief that individuals can be counted on to
pursue their own self-interest, which ultimately amounts to a
tendency to pursue maximum individual economic advantage. However,
the meaning of 'rationality' always emerges from oppositional play
with a notion of 'irrationality', and, in Schumpeter's case, the
"irrationality" against which 'rationality' is defined is, broadly, 'pur-

poselessness'. Thus, Schumpeter's rather restrictive definition of imperialism at the beginning of his essay ('an objectless disposition . . . to forcible expansion', Schumpeter, p. 6) has already consigned imperialism to the realm of 'irrational' behaviour even before he has demonstrated its economic irrationality by resort to historical evidence. His entire argument assumes the form of a tautological narrative in which the historical evidence is marshalled to defend a thesis which has already been clinched in the very beginning through the much tidier, if questionable, device of definition.

Leaving aside for the moment the question of how one can decide whether a particular enterprise is 'objectless' or not, for certainly all imperial adventures in history dating back to the time of Rameses II have been accompanied by propagandistic 'justifications' of the goals being sought, one can detect operating beneath the surface of Schumpeter's discourse a social class argument grounded in an historical metanarrative which posits the integration of a global 'free trade' order as the *telos* of world history. The economic meaning of imperialism, in Schumpeter's view, is free trade's evil opposite: export monopolism – an integrated imperial trading system with high tariff walls erected to exclude other developed trading economies. In what amounts to an updated inventorying of the Cobdenite argument against the Corn Laws, Schumpeter then lists the drawbacks to this kind of system: the protective tariffs necessitated by such a system confer full benefits only on large landowners; by imposing tariffs on imports, export monopolism harms small capitalists, workers, and consumers in the home country; while primary producers at home may stand to benefit in the short run, the industries which use their products will be forced to pay higher prices for basic commodities; export monopolism accelerates capital flight; and so on (Schumpeter, pp. 64-88). His conclusion – that export monopolies lead to greater anti-competitive concentration of domestic industry into trusts and cartels – converts his argument to a social class argument: a truly systematic 'imperial federation' would lead to a greater concentration of wealth in the hands of the few while inefficient industries would thrive. Since, on the other hand, free trade cannot promote the kind of industrial concentration which Hobson holds is the source of surplus finance capital, free trade capitalism cannot be responsible for the imperial policies of modern Europe (p. 88). Moreover, 'it is a basic fallacy to describe imperialism as a necessary phase of capitalism' (p. 89). *Pace* , Lenin.

Having thus deduced that it 'makes no sense' for capitalist societies to engage in 'The Great Game', Schumpeter is left with a large unanswered historical question: why have they? Moreover, why does Britain, the world's first industrialized society, possess the world's largest empire in 1919, an empire whose boundaries were greatly enlarged in the latter half of the nineteenth century?

The answer he offers has already been prepared for by his earlier discussion of ancient empires. Arguing that imperialism appeals to the 'dark powers of the subconscious', Schumpeter discovers a 'political unconscious' at work driving European nations into imperial adventures against their own better 'rational' judgement. His explanation, in short, is simultaneously sociological and psychological. Aristo-military castes, atavistic remnants of pre-capitalist relations of production – 'survivals', in effect – retain an excessive influence over political decision-making in Europe, at least partly by trumpeting expansionist policies based both on the exploitation of xenophobic fears of the alien and on the positive values of patriotic sacrifice for a cause larger than individual self-interest (pp. 64-5). Moreover, the European bourgeoisie, who should be able to resist transparently rhetorical appeals to imperial glory out of their own class interest, are nevertheless victims of 'mental patterning' by this pre-capitalist autocracy: thus, in most European countries they can be counted on, regrettably, to support policies of protectionism and imperial adventurism (p. 92). The European middle-classes, in other words, are subject to a 'dichotomy of attitudes and interests': their attitudes shaped by the influence of outdated militarism and jingoism; their interests determined by the needs of modern capitalism (p. 96).

Schumpeter's use of early popular 'Freudianism' is evident here – a 'Freudianism' which opposes higher-level 'rational' interest (heavily flavoured with political economy's notion of 'rationality') to lower-level 'irrational instinct'. Moreover, the hierarchical relationship between both poles of this dichotomy is essentially the same one which, in Freud's own work, was to harden gradually into the rigidly posed opposition of instinct to civilized rationality in *Civilization and its discontents* (1927). On this level of analysis, however, one must admire the psycho-sociological ambition of his analysis, however much havoc the dichotomy creates for his argument about the causes of imperialism.

On the other hand, it must be admitted that the very terms in which this psycho-sociological dichotomy is posed help to unsettle it. If

imperialism taps a libidinal reservoir of 'instincts' which have lost
their purpose in a modern capitalist world, and if capitalism absorbs
virtually all of a people's energies, leaving less and less room for the
exercise of these 'function-less' instincts (Schumpeter, p. 69), whence
comes the unquestionable explosion of imperial adventuring in which
Europe engaged in the decades preceding World War I? Imperialism
must tap a supplemental reservoir of cultural energy (Schumpeter, p.
27). But, if so, what is the meaning of the claim that capitalist
endeavour drains virtually the entire reservoir?

The logic Schumpeter deploys here is the logic of the Derridean
'supplement': he sees imperialism as culturally marginal, inefficient,
and 'irrational' in its aim, entering the capitalist order from outside
(p. 73) but answering to no need within capitalism, yet also the
essential motive force of modern history, the root cause of modern
wars. Imperialism is held to be simultaneously marginal and essential.
This is best revealed in Schumpeter's self-deconstructing closing
statement, in which he reveals that his point in writing the essay was
to 'demonstrate, by means of an important example, the ancient truth
that the dead always rule the living' (Schumpeter, p. 98). Schumpeter
does not seem aware of the implications of this statement, for if the
dead rule the living they cannot be 'dead', at least not in the usual
sense. Inspired by the Freudian 'repetition compulsion' with which
it is contemporary (Beyond the pleasure principle was written during the
same year), this claim is made by a man who cannot admit the
unsettling implications it holds for his attempt to marginalize
'aggressive' instincts and separate them from capitalism as a system.
Inscribed in the cultural unconscious to which they are consigned by
capitalism's rationality', atavistic militarist instincts surface in regret-
table form in order to write the deplorable modern history of Europe.
Like Haggard, whose repressive gestures at the end of She simply fold
the narrative back on itself by reinstating the conditions of inviting
mystery with which the novel began, Schumpeter's attempt to dismiss
'imperial instincts' as 'atavisms', to cast them into the hazardous waste
dump of history, simply guarantees that they will leech into the
ground water again to play their determinative role in a history always
already contaminated by economic 'irrationality'.

Schumpeter's attempt to vindicate capitalism's innocence has had
some important influence in the twentieth century. It emerges, for
instance, as the source of Ronald Robinson's and John Gallagher's
influential claim that 'official thinking in itself' may be the cause of

late nineteenth-century British imperialism.[10] Perhaps the best discussion of these issues in the post-World War II era, however, is contained in Hannah Arendt's *Origins of totalitarianism* (1951), a book which acknowledges its debt to some of Schumpeter's ideas but which is notably free of the overt repressive gestures which undermine the coherence of his argument. Writing in the immediate aftermath of the second and most destructive war among imperial competitors, Arendt adopts both Hobson's conclusion that surplus finance capital drove European nations to find outlets to absorb it overseas in the late Victorian era, and Schumpeter's definition of imperialism as 'aimless expansionism'. Arendt requires one to think the possibility that imperialism could be both aimless and purposeful simultaneously, and she arrives at that conclusion by carefully prying capitalist enterprise free from Schumpeter's more conventional notion of 'rational purposefulness'. What she adds to the debate over the connection between capitalism and empire, is a perceptive appreciation of the way both purpose and purposelessness are anomalously embodied in modern bureaucratic organization.

Arendt sees expansionism itself ('expansion for expansion's sake', Arendt, p. 126) as the most important historical legacy of the European bourgeoisie. Not only was the 'competition' essential to the effective functioning of Adam Smith's 'invisible hand' only possible when it was guaranteed by state power (Arendt, p. 126), but modern 'expansionism' is actually a 'business idea' which found its way into national politics when the European bourgeoisie recognized the economic necessity of expanding beyond the bounds of the nation-state:

Imperialism was born when the ruling class in capitalist production came up against national limitations to its economic expansion. The bourgeoisie turned to politics out of economic necessity; for if it did not want to give up the capitalist system whose inherent law is constant economic growth, it had to impose this law upon its home governments and to proclaim expansion to be an ultimate political goal of foreign policy. (Arendt, p. 126)

Acknowledging Seeley's point that the early British Empire had been acquired in a 'fit of absence of mind', she sees the colonial administrators of the Victorian era as engaged in turning this 'accident into a kind of willed act', retrospectively (Arendt, p. 207). The 'white man's burden' was invented to supply an instrumental purpose where none, in fact, existed. Thus, Kipling's central role as ideologist of imperialism: the 'Great Game' and the Secret Service invest empire with provisional, bureaucratic ends, purposes that enable and justify their instrumentality: they authorize manipulating others into doing the work of empire – the supreme satisfaction that bureaucratic management provides.

The examples she cites are Rhodes in South Africa and Cromer in Egypt: an interesting pairing because conventional wisdom usually draws a sharp distinction between the ruthlessly megalomaniacal Cape colony profiteer and the sober-minded rationalizer of British colonial administration in Egypt. Yet the superficial differences between the two melt away, under Arendt's analysis, because she emphasizes the crucial similarity of their bureaucratic positions: 'The outstanding similarity between Rhodes's rule in South Africa and Cromer's domination of Egypt was that both regarded the countries not as desirable ends in themselves but merely as means for some supposedly higher purpose' (Arendt, p. 212). In Rhodes' case, that end was simply 'unlimited expansion', for he reached the height of his influence in Africa after the Cape colony had ceased to serve any clear geopolitical function for the Indian empire. Cromer, by contrast, had to undergo a transition, for, initially posted to Egypt in 1883 when it had just acquired value as the 'road to India', he had to overcome his initial 'uneasiness' about being assigned an indefinite task in a land which Britain ruled in fact, but not by law (Arendt, p. 213). However, within a few years Cromer had begun to justify that 'hybrid form of government' and to prefer the power that 'personal influence', in the absence of clearly defined treaty obligations or geopolitical purposes, could offer. He had, in short, become a colonial bureaucrat: assembling a 'highly trained, highly reliable staff' whose loyalty and patriotism were not connected with personal ambition or vanity and who would even be required to renounce the human aspiration of having their names connected with their achievements' (Arendt, p. 213). Indeed, Cromer himself could become highly agitated when forced to come out of his 'hiding place' and acknowledge responsibility: he much preferred to remain behind the scenes pulling the strings.

The psychic appeal of this kind of rule, according to Arendt, lies in the anomalous combination of rewards it offers. While Rhodes felt himself a 'god' in the service of 'destiny' and Cromer, much more modestly, cast himself and his underlings as 'instruments of incomparable value' to the empire, the difference between 'instrument' and 'god' blurs under this technique of colonial management:

What overcame Rhodes's monstrous innate vanity and made him discover the charms of secrecy was the same thing that overcame Cromer's innate sense of duty: the discovery of an expansion which was not driven by the specific appetite for a specific country but conceived as an endless process in which every country would serve only as stepping-stone for further expansion. In view of such a concept, the desire for glory can no longer be satisfied by the glorious triumph over a specific people for the sake of one's own people, nor can the sense of duty be fulfilled through the consciousness of specific services and the fulfillment of specific tasks. No matter what individual qualities or defects a man may have, once he has entered the maelstrom of an unending process of expansion, he will, as it were, cease to be what he was and obey the laws of the process, identify himself with anonymous forces that he is supposed to serve in order to keep the whole process in motion; he will think of himself as mere function, and eventually consider such functionality, such an incarnation of the dynamic trend, his highest possible achievement. (Arendt, p. 215)

Encapsulated in this passage and held in logical tension is an insight into the connection between capitalism and empire that devolves on the notion of bureaucracy as self-perpetuating factory for the mass production of imperial goals. Cromer and Rhodes are bureaucrats ruling a system 'whose very essence is aimless process' (Arendt, p. 216), and whose pleasures derive both from boundless opportunity – it incarnates a bottomless imperial desire which is linked to the libidinal satisfaction offered by the expansionist tendency of modern capitalist enterprise, its tendency to endless substitution of satisfactions – and from submission, the pleasure of regarding oneself as instrument, as function, in service of something higher, the pleasure T. E. Lawrence so movingly describes. Arendt manages to trace the psychic springs of imperial management to their root in a desire that merges the megalomania of the ruler-god Kurtz with the imperial instrumentality of 'Our Man'—Nostromo. What the bureaucratic rule of late expansive capitalism does is to collapse the conventional boundary between matter and spirit by focusing bottomless desire on an object that is displaced just as one reaches for it. Moreover, it beckons with the promise of a transformation of subjectivity: master-slave, god-thing, the imperialist's self inhabits a space which cannot be confined within conventional categories. He is the puppeteer conceiving himself as the puppet of destiny, a 'destiny' which has actually been manufactured ad hoc to provide institutional motivation for the bureaucracy he both controls and serves. In what is now a familiar cyclical pattern characterizing the operation of military-industrial bureaucracies in advanced capitalist societies, the colonial bureaucracy of Cromer's day invents new colonial interests which it can then serve by expanding: it conceives itself the servant of an imperial destiny it masterfully manufactures.

As the revolution in Nostromo which separates Sulaco from Costaguana realizes Decoud's plan without any help from Decoud himself, who has no faith in it, colonial bureaucratic rule, in Arendt's view, is based in 'material interests' such as Nostromo – human beings as instruments serving ends embodied in 'plans', in 'intentions' independent of individual planners, in fact. In the presence of such 'intentions', one can dispense with the individual 'intender' (although not with the 'instrument') altogether because these intentions have been immortalized in institutions. Thus, Conrad's narrator, in that book, treats Captain Mitchell's post-revolutionary narrative with heavy irony precisely because Mitchell narrativizes the revolutionary experience through categories appropriate to individual initiative and derived from the literary code of romance. He reads 'heroism' and 'courage' into an historical event which is accidental in essence and, thus, one to which these categories barely apply. Narrativization requires a degree of intentionality to achieve coherence, yet the revolution in Sulaco can only be made to seem 'intentional' through retrospective narrativization: it must have been intended because it was accomplished; therefore, Decoud must have been the mastermind of Sulacan independence and Nostromo, the 'magnificent capataz de cargadores', its indispensable hero. In short, it assumes the form of a bourgeois individualist myth.

In its concern for this problematic retrospective construction of coherent narrative history out of the accident of actual historical experience, Nostromo offers striking insights into the psychic pleasures that accompany imperial bureaucratic rule that underscore Arendt's argument. One of Conrad's major themes here – the theme of human subjects as instruments, Nostromo as 'Our Man'—bears a striking resemblance to Arendt's discussion of the psychic satisfactions offered by Cromer's type of bureaucratic colonial rule. In fact, Conrad penetratingly examines the seemingly contradictory satisfactions conferred by the colonial bureaucrat's dual Hegelian position – master-slave, subject-object, god-thing – the promise of a transformation of subjectivity which imperial rule affords.

Although Nostromo is the most important functionary in this novel, all the main characters partake of this duality; all cast themselves at various points as actors on the stage of a destiny which is manufactured to fulfil the needs of the moment. Even Charles Gould, the character whose self-contained monomania seems to procure for him a measure of autonomy in this text, finds himself Holroyd's 'uomo' in Costaguana, although he is responsible for convincing Holroyd to invest in the mine in the first place. And Holroyd's motive in supporting the San Tomé mine is described in terms that evoke Arendt's Cromer as imperial administrator:

He was not running a great enterprise there; no mere railway board or industrial corporation. He was running a man! A success would have pleased him very much on refreshing novel grounds; but on the other side of the same feeling, it was incumbent upon him to cast it off utterly at the first sign of failure. A man may be thrown off.[11]

The pleasures of this kind of enterprise lie in reducing other human beings to instruments (the reduction of subjects to objects), while casting oneself in a compensatory role vis-à-vis 'destiny'. And, like Cromer, Holroyd prefers to 'run a man' while remaining behind the scenes, requiring no such satisfaction as the public identification with such a goal usually implies. His satisfaction, as Cromer's, comes from the deferral of satisfaction. Moreover, this transformation is symmetrical with another kind of transformation: the inflation of matter into symbol, of silver into a transcendental signified. In Conrad's Costaguana, the conventional European metaphysical opposition of idea and matter is problematized, rendered incapable of explaining motive. Thus, Mrs. Gould, in contemplating the significance of the first lump of silver which the mine produced, sublimates it:

she endowed that lump of metal with a justificative conception, as though it were not a mere fact, but something far-reaching and impalpable, like the true expression of an emotion or the emergence of a principle. (Nostromo, p. 98)

Moreover, the human instrument, Nostromo, the 'incorruptible capataz', is repeatedly conflated with that 'incorruptible' metal which he is charged with protecting.

Nostromo's plot eventually degenerates into personal tragedy resulting from the political stasis achieved by Sulaco after its revolution: no longer able to serve Decoud's plan once it has been realized, bereft of a 'dynamic trend' in history to which he can submit himself, in effect, deprived of a bureaucratic goal to serve, Nostromo chains his desire to the silver Decoud hid on the beach of Great Isabel and is, finally, undone in a tawdry operatic melodrama which closes his life at the hands of Viola – himself once a functionary of the great Garibaldi. Once a function – hero – in political romance, Nostromo assumes a different function – lover as victim – in a melodrama which is simply a recast romance plot, although Conrad's relentless irony will not allow his readers to lose sight of the fact that this melodramatic recuperation of Nostromo's plot distorts history by obscuring the fact that he was on Great Isabel to loot the silver. The imperial tragedy for which Nostromo's personal tragedy is a metonymy is the logical consequence of the static nature of Decoud's plan and, by extension, of the Europeans' 'plans' for Sulaco: independence for Sulaco is a finite goal. Once realized through Barrios's victory, the plan has nowhere to go. It dies in history because it does not suffer a sea-change into a bureaucracy capable of manufacturing, in effect, 'Cape-to-Cairo' railway schemes. The realization of a communal plan leaves its survivors deprived of any further reason for self-sacrifice, any purpose beyond the pursuit of the 'rational self-interest' that is the order of the day under capitalism.

Yet this pursuit of 'rational self-interest' can no longer be thought of as a species of simple 'materialism', for the silver from the San Tomé mine had already been transmuted into the 'symbol' of the 'material interests' during the Sulacan revolution, had already assumed the intersubjective status of signifier, of representation, of substitutive goal. Moreover the 'self' of 'self-interest' has been problematized here beyond recuperation within a metaphysical structure of subject and object. As Nostromo himself serves as currency throughout the main drama of the novel, loaned out to others who require the services of the incomparable 'instrument', his murder on Great Isabel re-establishes his humanity – only animate beings can be murdered – in the very moment when he is most closely identified with the 'incorruptible' currency he is stealing. Viola's act is equivalent to taking the currency of Sulaco out of circulation, to removing Nostromo from the historical process in which he was not so much an actor on its stage as a fold in its fabric.

The instability inherent in the historical dynamism of expansive capitalism, an instability which stems from capitalism's inherent tendency to excite bottomless desire and to transform subjectivity, is noted by Dr Monygham near the end of *Nostromo*. In response to Mrs. Gould's pathetic question 'Will there be never any peace?' Monygham replies:

'No!' interrupted the doctor. 'There is no peace and no rest in the development of material interests. They have their law, and their justice. But it is founded on expediency, and is inhuman; it is without rectitude, without the continuity and the force that can be found only in a moral principle. Mrs. Gould, the time approaches when all that the Gould Concession stands for shall weigh as heavily upon the people as the barbarism, cruelty, and misrule of a few years back.' (*Nostromo*, p. 406)

Dr Monygham deplores precisely what Cromer celebrates: an historical dynamic, a machine, is an engine powered by the idea of expansion for its own sake, but larger and infinitely more powerful than the individual subject, which it converts into a function to supply its continuing dynamism. Founded in bottomless desire, it relies for its effectiveness on an infinite deferral of satisfaction, an infinite supplementation of alternative goals. Located in the imperial sphere, it no longer, by the twentieth century, makes any sense to try and distinguish this 'machine' from formal government or imperial armies. This is the historical dynamic of capitalist imperialism.

Notes

Preface

1 Gayatri Spivak has recently argued the necessity of rereading 'domestic' Victorian culture in light of the central importance of the imperial project. Her 'imperial' reading of *Jane Eyre* points in a direction which this book develops. Gayatri Chakravorty Spivak, 'Three Women's Texts and a Critique of Imperialism', in *'Race', Writing, and Difference*, ed. Henry Louis Gates, Jr. (Chicago: University of Chicago Press, 1987), pp. 262-80.

Chapter 1

1 Portions of Chapter 1 appeared under the title 'Disraeli's political trilogy and the antinomic structure of imperial desire' in *Novel*, 22/3 (Spring 1989), pp. 305-25.

2 Robert Blake describes it as 'the biggest instalment of social reform passed by any one government in the nineteenth century'. Robert Blake, *Disraeli* (London: Eyre and Spottiswoode, 1966), p. 553. On Disraeli's contribution on promoting the emotional appeal of empire, see A. P. Thornton, *The imperial idea and its enemies* (New York: St. Martin's, 1963), p. xiii.

3 Levine states Disraeli's position thus: 'Mankind moves constantly upward, as it were, from the Middle Ages and before; but in order for this movement to be successful, it not only must be based on the great principles of the past but must be forever refining and reinterpreting those principles for its own time.' Richard A. Levine, *Benjamin Disraeli* (New York: Twayne, 1968), p. 90.

4 Quoted in Alan Sandison, *The wheel of empire* (New York: St. Martin's, 1967), p. 57.

5 Thomas Carlyle, *Sartor Resartus* (New York: Doubleday, 1937).

6 Friedrich Nietzsche, *Beyond good and evil*, trans. Walter Kaufmann (New York: Vintage, 1966), p. 160.

7 Benjamin Disraeli, *Coningsby, Sybil, and Tancred*, vols. XII-XVI of *The works of Benjamin Disraeli, Earl of Beaconsfield* (New York: Walter Dunne, 1904), vol. XII, p. xvi.

8 Geoffrey H. Hartman, 'Romanticism and antiself-consciousness', *Romanticism: points of view*, eds. Robert F. Gleckner and Gerald E. Enscoe, 2nd edn. (Detroit: Wayne State University Press, 1975), p. 290.

9 This is essentially what Jeffrey Mehlman does in his book *Repetition and revolution*, where he argues that repetition 'collapses' history because history is nothing but the 'serial ordering of the novel'. Jeffrey Mehlman, *Repetition and revolution* (Berkeley: University of California Press, 1977), p. 12.

10 That Freud was to come around eventually to the belief that the 'primal scene' can never truly be 're-experienced' is clear in his famous letter to Fliess, dated 21 September 1897. As Jean Laplanche summarizes its significance, 'Freud proposes, in opposition to his own theory, objections of fact – the impossibility of ever rediscovering the "scene" – and of principle: the impossibility of admitting that paternal perversion is that frequent and, above all, the inability to decide whether a scene discovered in analysis is true or

fantasied.' Jean Laplanche, *Life and death in psychoanalysis*, trans. Jeffrey Mehlman (Baltimore: Johns Hopkins, 1976), p. 32.

11 Edmund Leach, 'The legitimacy of Solomon', *Introduction to structuralism*, ed. Michael Lane (New York: Basic, 1970: 248-92), p. 252.

12 'School' is the source or ground of representations as well as a representation of an anterior original moment, a reflection. 'In this play of representation, the point of origin becomes ungraspable. There are things, like reflecting pools, and images, an infinite reference from one to the other, but no longer a source, a spring. There is no longer a simple origin. For what is reflected is split in *itself* and not only as an addition to itself of its image. The reflection, the image, the double, splits what it doubles. The origin of the speculation becomes a difference. What can look at itself is not one; and the law of the addition of the origin to its representation, of the thing to its image, is that one plus one makes at least three.' Jacques Derrida, *Of grammatology*, trans. Gayatri Chakravorty Spivak (Baltimore: Johns Hopkins, 1976), pp. 36-7.

13 See Lord Blake: 'Young England was the Oxford movement translated by Cambridge from religion into politics', a revulsion from 'Liberal utilitarianism'. R. Blake, p. 171.

14 Daniel R. Schwarz notes that all three novels of the trilogy impose upon their protagonists the task of 're-educating' themselves. Daniel R. Schwarz, *Disraeli's fiction* (London: Macmillan, 1979), p. 86. More in line with my contention, though, is Brantlinger's claim that Disraeli seeks to establish the illusory nature of the 'two nations' theory by having his protagonists discover the diversity of the class system in England. Patrick Brantlinger, 'Tory radicalism and "The two nations" in Disraeli's Sybil', *Victorian newsletter*, 41 (Spring 1972), pp. 13-17.

15 Nietzsche asserts that all moralities spring from the opposition of exterior and interior, 'we' and 'they'. The function of the dangerous exteriorized class is to give one a focus for projecting feelings of 'power' and 'dangerousness'. As he argues: 'into evil one's feelings project power and dangerousness, a certain terribleness, subtlety, and strength that does not permit contempt to develop. According to slave morality, those who are "evil" thus inspire fear; according to master morality it is precisely those who are "good" that inspire, and wish to inspire, fear, while the "bad" are felt to be contemptible.' Friedrich Nietzsche, *Beyond good and evil*, trans. Walter Kaufmann (New York: Vintage, 1966), p. 207.

16 Robert Blake (p. 191) faults Disraeli for proposing a revival of monarchical power as a 'panacea' for England's social ills. However, as I hope this discussion has made clear, Disraeli's interest in 'mediating' figures goes far beyond merely singling out the monarchy for praise; his purpose in inventing the 'mediating' class is precisely to mystify origins which spring from opposition – the subjection of one class to another.

Like his mentor Burke, Disraeli believes in the necessity of 'cloaking' the naked exercise of power in the garb of civilization. In one of his more eloquent passages, Burke laments the tendency of the French Revolution to strip away that which is both necessary and supplementary about civilization: 'All the pleasing illusions, which made power gentle, and obedience liberal, which harmonized the different shades of life, and which, by a bland assimilation, incorporated into politics the sentiments which beautify and soften private society, are to be dissolved by this new conquering empire of light and reason. All the decent drapery of life is to be rudely torn off. All the superadded ideas, furnished from the wardrobe of a moral imagination, which the heart owns, and the understanding ratifies, as necessary to cover the defects of our naked shivering nature, and to raise it to dignity in our own estimation, are to be exploded as a ridiculous, absurd, and antiquated fashion.' Edmund Burke, *Reflections on the revolution in France* (London: Penguin, 1979), p. 171.

17 Nils Clausson notes how the later Disraeli was to lose his nostalgic fondness for Roman Catholicism, a turn in his allegiances evident from his tarring of Cardinal Manning with the brush of papist allegiances in *Lothair*. Nils Clausson, 'English Catholics and Roman

Catholicism in Disraeli's novels', *Nineteenth-century fiction*, 33 (1979), p. 455.

18 Quoted in Cecil Roth, *Benjamin Disraeli, Earl of Beaconsfield* (New York: Philosophical Library, 1952), p. 64.

19 See Jacques Derrida, *Margins of philosophy*, trans. Alan Bass (Chicago: University of Chicago, 1982), p. 20.

20 Sigmund Freud, *Totem and taboo*, trans. A. A. Brill (New York: Random House, 1946), pp. 189-98. Freud argues that the feast itself is originally an attempt by the 'brothers' to 'sanctify' themselves by partaking of the 'totem meal' – ultimately nothing but a gesture of identification with the father whom they had killed in the primal parricide. A result of this communal meal is the erection of a patriarchal order which no longer requires an existent father to enforce its rules, for those rules have been introjected by the brothers who have elevated the dead father to the role of punishing god.

21 Not surprisingly, Eva is drawn with courtly love trappings: her attractiveness is proportional to her unavailability, and she is, at one point, celebrated in song by a Bedouin 'troubadour' as his object of selfless devotion. *Tancred*, p.180.

22 Edward Said's *Orientalism* is an indispensable guide to the 'Romantic redemptive fantasies' that structure a great deal of 'orientalist' literature. As Said argues, the impulse behind the orientalist 'reinterpretation' of the East is often a need to restore it to the 'present' (one might add, without distortion, to restore 'presence'): 'Most of the time, not surprisingly, this interpretation is a form of Romantic restructuring of the Orient, a re-vision of it, which restores it redemptively to the present.' Edward Said, *Orientalism* (New York: Vintage, 1979), p. 158.

Tancred's Lebanese adventures provide powerful evidence of Disraeli's inability to write 'pure romance' unadulterated by practical political concerns. As Said remarks: '*Tancred* is not merely an Oriental lark but an exercise in the astute political management of actual forces on actual territories' (p. 169). However, one might wish to temper such a claim with the obvious reminder that the 'actual forces' Disraeli seeks to manage are themselves already romanticized versions of medieval feudal English 'forces'. Disraeli's political instincts are astute, but his Tancred is nevertheless mired in a Lebanon of his own making.

23 Alfred Bercovici, *That blackguard Burton!* (New York: Bobbs-Merrill, 1962), p. 102.

24 For a much fuller discussion of this history, see George Stocking, Jr., *Victorian anthropology* (New York: Macmillan, 1987), pp. 8-77.

25 See Said, pp. 123-48 and Stocking, pp. 68-9.

26 Lawrence, T. E. *Seven pillars of wisdom* (New York: Doubleday, 1935). The work which raises the most disturbing questions about the historical accuracy of Lawrence's account of his own role is Suleiman Mousa, *T. E. Lawrence: an Arab view* (New York and London: Oxford University Press, 1966).

27 'Servitude, like other conduct, was profoundly modified to Eastern minds by their obsession with the antithesis between flesh and spirit. These lads took pleasure in subordination; in degrading the body: so as to throw into greater relief their freedom in equality of mind: almost they preferred servitude as richer in experience than authority, and less binding in daily care.

  Consequently the relation of master and man in Arabia was at once more free and more subject than I had experienced elsewhere. Servants were afraid of the sword of justice and of the steward's whip, not because the one might put an arbitrary term to their existence, and the other print red rivers of pain about their sides, but because these were the symbols and the means to which their obedience was vowed. They had a gladness of abasement, a freedom of consent to yield to their master the last service and degree of their flesh and blood, because their spirits were equal with his and the contract voluntary. Such boundless engagement precluded humiliation, repining and regret.' Lawrence, p. 466.

Chapter 2

1 Richard Cobden was the most important Victorian defender of the 'anti-imperialist, free trade' position. To him, Britain's empire was largely an unwarranted drain on the national treasury, superfluous to maintaining her pre-eminent position in the world which, he argued, stemmed solely from her manufacturing prowess: 'our national existence is involved in the well-doing of our manufacturers. If our readers ... should ask, ... To what are we indebted for this commerce? – we answer, in the name of every manufacturer and merchant of the kingdom – The *cheapness* alone of our manufactures. Are we asked, How is this trade protected, and by what means can it be enlarged? The reply still is, By the *cheapness* of our manufactures. Is it inquired how this mighty industry, upon which depends the comfort and existence of the whole empire, can be torn from us? – we rejoin, Only by the *greater cheapness* of the manufactures of another country.' Richard Cobden, *The political writings of Richard Cobden*, vol. I (London: Fisher Unwin, 1903; reprinted New York: Kraus, 1969), p. 219.

2 Benjamin Disraeli, 'Crystal Palace speech' (24 June 1872), *Selected speeches*, ed. T. E. Kebbel (London: Longmans, Green & Co.,1882), p. 534.

3 The Victorian explorer-missionary David Livingstone helped create a popular interest in the African continent by convincing Britons that the promotion of 'Christianity and commerce' there was part of Britain's moral mission (and also might be quite profitable): 'By encouraging the native propensity for trade, the advantages that might be derived in a commercial point of view are incalculable; nor should we lose sight of the inestimable blessings it is in our power to bestow upon the unenlightened African, by giving him the light of Christianity. Those two pioneers of civilization – Christianity and commerce – should ever be inseparable; and Englishmen should be warned by the fruits of neglecting that principle as exemplified in the result of the management of Indian Affairs.' This particular sermon was delivered in the immediate aftermath of the 'Indian Mutiny' in 1858. David Livingstone, *Dr. Livingstone's Cambridge lectures* (Cambridge: Deighton, Bell and Co., 1858), p. 21.

4 This is essentially what Martin Green does in a recent book on the literature of colonialism. He locates a contest for supremacy between an 'aristo-military caste' and a 'bourgeois caste' in the adventure literature emerging in the England of the eighteenth through the twentieth centuries. Martin Green, *Dreams of adventure, deeds of empire* (New York: Basic, 1979), pp. 15-27.

5 The modern debate over the role of bourgeois culture in encouraging imperial expansion has been raging since the late nineteenth century. Although Conrad's *Heart of darkness* depicts very clearly an insidious kind of commercial imperialism operating in the Congo of the 1890s, the academic 'economic' debate proper really begins with the publication of J. A. Hobson's *Imperialism: a study* at the turn of the century (1902). For a fuller discussion of this issue, see the Postscript.

6 In one of his most politically costly offhand remarks, made while he was feeling the pressure of Gladstone's 'Midlothian' campaign against his pro-Turkish foreign policy, Disraeli referred to 'Mr. Gladstone's speech' attacking Turkey for massacring scores of Bulgarian Christians as the 'greatest Bulgarian atrocity' (R. Blake, p. 593). In this regard, it is worth noting that the political success of Gladstone's notoriously moralistic 'Midlothian' campaign testifies to the degree to which the language of Evangelical moralism had become (by the late 1870s) the language which formed the middle-class experience of the imperial enterprise.

7 J. Huizinga, *Homo ludens*, trans. anonymous (London: Routledge and Kegan Paul, 1949), p. 65.

8 The universality of this dichotomy is questioned by Jacques Ehrmann in an interesting rereading of Huizinga's *Homo ludens* from 1968. Ehrmann argues that the distinction, which might seem to carry all the weighty authority of 'intuition', is actually a quite

recently contrived opposition which corresponds to the materialist/idealist metaphysics underpinning the early industrial phase of Western civilization. Jacques Ehrmann, 'Homo ludens revisited', *Yale French studies*, 41 (1968), p. 46. In deconstructing Huizinga's *Homo ludens*, Ehrmann makes the important observation that the application of this distinction to other cultures constitutes an ethnocentrism of the worst sort: 'if play as the capacity for symbolization and ritualization is consubstantial with culture, it cannot fail to be present wherever there is culture. We realize then that play cannot be defined as a luxury. Whether their stomachs are full or empty, men play because they are men. 'To say that play "implies leisure" is to set forth the problem while placing oneself in an ethnocentric perspective that falsifies the basic data to be analyzed: it is to oppose the notion of work to that of leisure (an opposition which carries with it all the others we have already noted: utility-gratuitousness, seriousness-play, etc.). Such an opposition may be valid in our society (and even there, less and less), but it certainly cannot be generalized to include cultures other than our own.'

9 Martin Green's work contains a very useful discussion of the evolution of boys' adventure literature in Victorian Britain. Green, pp. 203-33.

10 H. Rider Haggard, *King Solomon's mines* (New York: Puffin, 1983).

11 Brian V. Street, *The savage in literature* (London: Routledge and Kegan Paul, 1975), p. 83.

12 Sir Richard Burton, *Personal narrative of a pilgrimage to El-Medinah and Mecca* (New York: Putnam, 1856). Burton played a variety of notorious roles in his public life: one of them was the role of amateur anthropologist. He was the original vice-president of Hunt's Anthropological Society, and his role at meetings is described by Burrow as involving 'airing his distaste for negroes and rejoicing in the rising value of phallic specimens among European collectors'. J. W. Burrow, *Evolution and society: a study in Victorian social theory* (Cambridge: Cambridge University Press, 1966), p. 125.

13 Edward Said makes a point of noting Burton's 'preternatural' appreciation of the way social life is structured by codes in *Orientalism* (p.195). Much of what I have to say was originally suggested by Said's analysis of Burton, although he does not make a point of noting how the demands of disguise contribute, not only to Burton's view of human cultures as code-governed structures, but also to his notions of national identity as nodes in a network of differences.

14 As Said notes, Burton was in rebellion against conventional Victorian moral codes. Said, p. 190.

15 Thus, Derrida cites Lévi-Strauss's discovery of what he calls the 'scandal' of the incest prohibition: a discovery which reveals that the nature/culture opposition inheres, not in the external world, but in the conceptual structure – the intellectual tools – which anthropologists use to attempt to make sense of that world. *Writing and difference*, p. 284.

16 Burton's confusing position is complicated by his overuse of the nineteenth-century umbrella term 'race', amalgamating notions of linguistic, cultural, biological, and geographical identity. While most twentieth-century anthropologists attempt to distinguish sharply between the cultural, linguistic, geographical (and ultimately political) concept of 'nationality' and the biological notion of 'race', Burton makes such distinctions only haphazardly and usually accidentally. Thus, while one might assume that he implicitly acknowledges 'essential' differences between European 'races' and Muslim 'races' but only 'non-essential' differences between different Muslim cultural groups, the book does not at all make this clear (moreover this is complicated by his apparent adoption of certain conventional Arab cultural prejudices to furnish the wardrobe of disguise). Moreover, his dual role as both 'scientific' observer of alien societies and self-exiled critic of Victorian English ethnocentric complacency complicates the issue mightily. He seems to rely on essentialist notions of race and nationality only when these suit the polemical purposes of the moment, meanwhile challenging his readers to identify sympathetically with his position – the man whose social identity is constructed by different social codes – when he finds it convenient to score his more

'relativistic' points.

17 E. M. Forster, *A passage to India* (New York and London: Harcourt Brace Jovanovich, 1924).

18 Steven Marcus, 'Stalky & co.', in *Kipling and the critics*, ed. Elliot L. Gilbert (London: Peter Owen, 1966), p. 161.

19 Rudyard Kipling, *Kim* (New York: Doubleday, 1926). If it has not been made clear already let me reiterate that by 'motivelessness' I do not mean to imply that there is 'no motive' behind imperial desire but rather that what motives there are are riven by contradiction – incoherent motives. Nor do I mean to imply that, say, Disraeli's *Tancred* can ever be cited as proof of the absurd proposition that England engaged in a world-wide process of imperial incorporation for what are essentially playful purposes. Disraeli's purpose in endowing his hero with 'playful' motives is clearly ideological: he masks the truth by offering the game of empire as a field for the exercise of impulses that one is bound to describe as 'playful' because they have been designed not to *appear* to serve ulterior political purposes.

20 Wittgenstein's notion of 'language games' casts some light on what I am getting at here. Once one begins to look at human behaviour as governed by rule structures, one quickly finds that the distinction between game-like rule structures and others based on presumably 'serious' assumptions is untenable. For one thing, some games are 'serious'; others are less so. Moreover, Wittgenstein uses the term 'game' to embrace all rule-governed activity because he comes to the compelling conclusion that he is ultimately in no position to judge whether or not any particular rule-system serves 'serious' or 'playful' purposes. Ludwig Wittgenstein, *Philosophical investigations I*, trans. G. E. M. Anscombe (New York and London: Macmillan, 1958), pp. 31^e-32^e.

21 Kipling was heavily influenced by the English public school ethos. His book *Stalky and co.*, one of the classic British schoolboy novels, is set in the United Services College at Westward Ho! and his hero, Stalky, is, like Kim, unconventional and rebellious, although ultimately this rebelliousness is channelled in a direction useful to the empire. Rudyard Kipling, *Stalky and co.* (New York: Doubleday, 1927). A novel of rebellion within clearly defined limits, *Stalky* reveals Kipling's need to see all rebellion as ultimately serving the paradoxical goal of restoring equipoise and affirming law. As Philip Mason argues, this explains Kipling's being 'always on the side of the Head but often against the housemaster'. Philip Mason, *Kipling: the glass, the shadow, and the fire* (New York: Harper and Row, 1975), pp. 45-6.

22 This is one dimension to what Irving Howe calls Kipling's 'vision of ultimate goodness or harmony'. Irving Howe, 'Editor's introduction', *The portable Kipling* (New York: Viking, 1982), p. xxii. After having written this chapter, I discovered an analysis of Kim which suggests, in general outline, some of the approach taken here. See Abdul R. JanMohamed, 'The economy of Manichean allegory: the function of racial difference in colonialist literature', in *'Race', writing, and difference*, ed. Henry Louis Gates, Jr. (Chicago and London: University of Chicago Press, 1986), pp. 96-100.

23 On Kipling's notion of 'Law', see Shamsul Islam, *Kipling's 'law': a study of his philosophy of life* (London: Macmillan, 1975).

24 Kipling is 'first and foremost the poet of work'. C. S. Lewis, 'Kipling's world', *Kipling and the critics*, ed. Elliot L. Gilbert (London: Peter Owen, 1966), p. 102. Contrast this claim with Hannah Arendt's very different observation that 'purposelessness is the very charm of Kim's existence'. Hannah Arendt, *The origins of totalitarianism* (New York: Harcourt Brace, 1958), p. 217. In fact, viewing English imperialism as basically 'aimless expansionism', Arendt notes how England erected a bureaucratic system of colonial rule which tended to 'infantilize' British values generally: 'Strange and curious lands attracted the best of England's youth since the end of the nineteenth century, deprived her society of the most honest and the most dangerous elements, and guaranteed, in addition to this bliss, a certain conservation, or perhaps petrification of boyhood

noblesse which preserved *and* infantilized Western moral standards' (p. 185). See the Postscript for a fuller discussion of Arendt's views.

25 See Dodgson's references to his puzzle in letters to Mrs. J. G. Church and R. H. Collins in 1893. Charles Luttwidge Dodgson, *The letters of Lewis Carroll*, vol. II, ed. Morton N. Cohen (New York: Oxford University Press, 1979), pp. 962 and 970. What follows first appeared under the title 'Alice the child-imperialist and the games of wonderland', in *Nineteenth-century literature* (September 1986), pp. 143-71.

26 Lewis Carroll, *Alice's adventures in Wonderland, the annotated Alice*, introduction and notes by Martin Gardner (New York: NAL, 1964). I am extrapolating Richard Rorty's notion of 'incommensurable discourses' here by applying it to Alice's failed attempt to 'read' the meaning of the 'creatures'' words and actions by imposing an interpretive schema which is nothing other than her own English conventionality hypostatized into a metasystem or metalanguage. In *Philosophy and the mirror of nature*, Rorty argues that 'epistemology' performs an analogous trick by attempting to render all discourses translatable through imposing its own set of favoured terms: 'there is no such thing as the "language of unified science". We have not got a language which will serve as a permanent neutral matrix for formulating all good explanatory hypotheses, and we have not the foggiest notion of how to get one. ... So epistemology – as the attempt to render all discourses commensurable by translating them into a preferred set of terms – is unlikely to be a useful strategy.' Richard Rorty, *Philosophy and the mirror of nature* (Princeton, NJ: Princeton University Press, 1979), pp. 348-9.

  Many critics have discussed Lewis Carroll's obsession with rules and rule-governed behaviour. Indeed, one might argue that some of the best criticism of *Alice's adventures in Wonderland* has focused on his interest in games and play, whether it be Kathleen Blake's discussion of the play/work dichotomy (both of which spheres of experience Carroll is said to place in a rule-governed context) or Roger Henkle's identification of Carroll's timid proposal of 'free play' as an alternative to a mid-Victorian life of stultifying, repressive work. Kathleen Blake, *Play, games, and sport: the literary works of Lewis Carroll* (Ithaca, NY: Cornell University Press, 1974), p. 88; Roger B. Henkle, 'The Mad Hatter's world', *Virginia quarterly review*, 49/1 (1974), pp. 102-3.

  The standard work treating the creatures as spokesmen for various sorts of nonsense is Elizabeth Sewell's *The field of nonsense* (London: Chatto and Windus, 1952). An interesting contemporary discussion is contained in Susan Stewart's *Nonsense: aspects of intertextuality in folklore and literature* (Baltimore: Johns Hopkins University Press, 1979). In contrast to Sewell's view, my position is that what appears to be 'nonsense' in *Alice* may simply be 'sense' of an alien kind.

  Lest it be objected that I am overlooking the obvious fact that the 'creatures' speak 'English' words here, it is worth making the point that such may simply be Carroll's concession to the needs of an English-speaking readership. After all, no modern viewer of a Hollywood World War II film mistakes the Japanese soldiers depicted in it for Americans simply because the director has them speaking English.

27 Play, games, and sport is by far the best critical discussion of play as mastery in Carroll. Relying especially on Piaget and Huizinga, Blake sees play as an active drive to incorporate: 'play – spontaneous, disinterested, nonutilitarian – is characterized by a fundamental urge to mastery through incorporation of experience to the ego rather than by adjustment or accommodation of the ego to experience.' K. Blake, p. 18. This definition, oddly enough, disqualifies much of Alice's experience in Wonderland from inclusion in the realm of play: Alice's attempts to master the 'creatures' by inferring the rules governing their 'games' are thwarted at almost every turn, even though her growth spurts do afford her occasional opportunities to bully the 'creatures'. However, bullying is hardly what Blake means by playing the game here.

  In fact, the assumption of a 'mastery urge' leads Blake to infer that it is possible to distinguish Alice's being 'in the game' from being 'outside the game' and her 'playing' the game from 'being played by' the game (see K. Blake, pp. 69-70), as well as those moments when she masters her experience by incorporating it from those when she is mastered or incorporated by it (K. Blake, pp. 18-19). However, the book offers no such guideposts for its readers. Not only does *Alice* subvert facilely ethnocentric distinctions between 'game' and 'life', but, moreover, any attempt to exclude ritual from the discussion of play and games in this text requires one to buy into a number of questionable assumptions that Alice herself makes. Blake is ultimately placed in the ethnocentric positions Ehrmann identifies: attempting to read *Alice* by the categories inherited from the very recent history of the West, categories which the book itself 'masterfully' calls into question.

28 *Through the looking-glass* very clearly raises without answering the question of what sort of controlling rationality governs Alice's 'moves' on the chessboard. Roger B. Henkle, 'Carroll's narratives underground: "modernism" and form', in *Lewis Carroll: a celebration*, ed. Edward Guiliano (New York: Clarkson, 1982), pp. 92-3.

29 See the OED definition of its use in England: 'In English newspapers since 1878, generally misused, and applied opprobriously to a committee or organization charged with seeking to manage the elections and dictate to the constituencies, but which is, in fact, usually a representative committee popularly elected for the purpose of securing concerted political action in a constituency.' *The compact edition of the Oxford English dictionary* (Oxford: Oxford University Press, 1971), p. 191.

Obviously, the popular nineteenth-century British view of the meaning of the word is evoked here on the level of appearances: the Dodo does seem to stage-manage the 'race'. However, my point is simply that because Alice lacks an interpretive framework that would enable her to judge whether or not the 'creatures' are actually improvising when they appear to be (there obviously is no universal code that allows people to make definitive judgements about whether inhabitants of foreign cultures they know nothing about are improvising or strictly following rigid rules laid down in antiquity), the American sense of the word 'caucus' offers itself as one plausible sense of the word 'caucus' here, especially in light of the other compelling evidence against assimilating the Wonderland 'caucus-race' to the English notion of a 'race'.

30 The two best critical studies of the Alice books to insist on the possibly 'logical' (i.e. 'rule-governed') basis for the 'creatures" behaviour are George Pitcher's 'Wittgenstein, nonsense, and Lewis Carroll', *Massachusetts review*, 6/3 (1965), pp. 591-611 and Patricia Meyer Spacks' 'Logic and language in *Through the looking-glass*', *Aspects of Alice*, ed. Robert Phillips (New York: Vintage, 1977), pp. 267-75. Pitcher usefully notes that the text foregrounds Alice's problems of rule inference while demonstrating that Carroll plays with notions analagous to the 'language-games' of which Wittgenstein would write years later, although he is not concerned in this essay with attempting to recuperate any of the 'creatures" games as 'sensible'. In her essay, Spacks argues that Carroll satirizes, through Alice, the illogical everyday use of language, or perhaps more appropriately, the illogicality of those who, like Alice, attempt to fit everyday language to the demands of logical rigour.

See also Gilles Deleuze, 'The schizophrenic and language: surface and depth in Lewis Carroll and Antonin Artaud', *Perspectives in post-structuralist criticism*, ed. and trans. Josue V. Harari (Ithaca, NY: Cornell University Press, 1979), for the interesting contrast he draws between Carroll's stark depiction of the linguistic 'surface' and Artaud's 'howl', which defeats all attempts to recuperate it within a linguistic system of meaning. As Deleuze argues, 'Without this surface that distinguishes itself from the depths of bodies, without this line that separates things from propositions, sounds would become inseparable from bodies, becoming simple physical qualities contiguous with them, and propositions would be impossible. This is why *the organization of language is not separable from the poetic discovery of surface*, or from Alice's adventure. The greatness of language consists in speaking only at the surface of things, and thereby in capturing the pure event and the combinations of events that take place on the surface. It becomes a question of reascending to the surface, of discovering surface entities and their games of meaning and of non-sense, of expressing these games in portmanteau words, and of resisting the vertigo of the bodies' depths and their alimentary, poisonous mixtures' (pp. 284-5).

31 'Self-consciousness exists in itself and for itself, in that, and by the fact that it exists for another self-consciousness; that is to say, it is only by being acknowledged or recognized.' G. W. F. Hegel, *The phenomenology of mind*, trans. J. B. Baillie (New York: Harper and Row, 1967), p. 229.

32 Self-consciousness is the next step: for instance, the philosopher's realization that it is *he* who 'comprehends' Napoleon.

33 The master 'exists only for himself, that is his essential nature; he is the negative power without qualification, a power to which the thing is naught. And he is thus the absolutely essential act in this situation, while the bondsman is not so, he is an unessential activity. But for recognition proper there is needed the moment that what the master does to the other he should also do to himself, and what the bondsman does to himself, he should do to the other also. On that account a form of recognition has arisen that is one sided and unequal.

'In all this, the unessential consciousness is, for the master, the object which embodies the truth of his certainty of himself. But it is evident that this object does not correspond to its notion; for, just where the master has effectively achieved lordship, he really finds that something has come about quite different from an independent consciousness. It is not an independent, but rather a dependent consciousness that he has achieved. He is thus not assured of self-existence as his truth; he finds that his truth is rather the unessential consciousness, and the fortuitous unessential action of that consciousness.' Hegel, pp. 236-7.

34 Thus, the French colonialists in Africa were able to attain a relatively stable position of imperial authority over the Malagasy, at least for a time, because of what seemed to be an oddly complementary psycho-cultural meshing of widely different social codes. One of the most influential European attempts to explain this is to be found in Octave Mannoni's *Prospero and Caliban*, trans. Pamela Powesland (New York: Praeger, 1964). According to Mannoni, a European treats an objective position of dependence as a sign of inferiority while a Malagasy only feels inferior when 'the bonds of dependence are in some way threatened' (p. 40). Needless to say, this implies that once they had imposed their authority by superior force, the French colonialists necessarily were able to 'discover' plenty of evidence of Malagasy 'inferiority'. The true threat to French rule came only in the twentieth century, and its initial source was the French-educated Malagasies who had been exiled to a system which rewards oedipal autonomy. On the other hand, the 'orphaned' state of modern Occidental adults (God in his heaven, not on earth) creates a psychological state of intolerable anxiety for the traditional Malagasy tribesman who has been raised to value a dependence relationship with a personalized authority (p. 59).

While Mannoni's explanations cast important light on Europeans' sense of their transaction with non-Western people in the imperial field, provided one reads 'under' his argument as I have done here, one needs to be suspicious of his rather ahistorical use of "Oedipal" models for the reasons cited above. Frantz Fanon questions his approach on these grounds in his critique of Mannoni, 'The so-called dependency complex of colonized peoples', in *Black skins, white masks*, trans. Charles Lam Markmann (New York: Grove Press, 1967), pp. 83-108.

35 Thus, as Mannoni argues, although one culture can never adequately interpret another culture's experience, the imperial attempt to dominate does sometimes create its own self-ratifying conditions which exist either in spite of or because of the lack of adequate inter-cultural understanding (for instance, as mentioned above, the European need to

exercise authority produces the appearance of submission by a colonized people who are then held to have demonstrated by that fact their 'need' to be ruled). Mannoni, p. 24.

36 In the *Introductory lectures* of 1917, Freud acknowledges not only the existence but the therapeutic necessity of transferential relationships between doctor and patient. Acknowledging that once the doctor comes to play an important role in the patient's drama(s) his ability to influence the patient's 'intellectual beliefs' (as opposed to the root cause of his illness) by simple 'suggestion' is greatly enhanced, Freud argues that the doctor must work to extract himself sufficiently from the transference so that he will eschew these 'easy' interpretive 'successes' and draw the patient's conscious attention to the fact that he is playing a role in his drama: 'We look upon successes that set in too soon as obstacles rather than as a help to the work of analysis; and we put an end to such successes by constantly resolving the transference on which they are based. It is this last characteristic which is the fundamental distinction between analytic and purely suggestive therapy, and which frees the results of analysis from the suspicion of being successes due to suggestion. In every other kind of suggestive treatment the transference is carefully preserved and left untouched; in analysis it is itself subjected to treatment and is dissected in all the shapes in which it appears. At the end of an analytic treatment the transference must itself be cleared away; and if success is then obtained or continues, it rests, not on suggestion, but on the achievement by its means of an overcoming of internal resistances, on the internal change that has been brought about in the patient.' Sigmund Freud, *Introductory lectures*, trans. and ed. James Strachey (New York: Norton, 1966), p. 453. Thus, the analyst must rise 'above' the transferential relationship to the extent of bringing it to the patient's attention and subjecting it to criticism.

37 Note the privilege Hegel accords himself in the *Phenomenology*: he is the 'Wise Man' because he writes at the 'end' of history, comprehending the deeds of the world-historical figure Napoleon. This is the privilege of the interpreter of a narrative: beyond the point of closure, one can cast previous events into meaningful order – as events 'leading up to' the end – in Hegel's case, the moment of writing the *Phenomenology*. Alexandre Kojève, *Introduction to the reading of Hegel*, assembled by Raymond Queneau, ed. Allan Bloom, trans. James H. Nichols, Jr. (New York: Basic, 1969), pp. 34-5.

See the somewhat analogous argument in Peter Brooks' 'Repetition, repression, and return: *Great expectations* and the study of plot'. Examining Freud's *Beyond the pleasure principle* as an implicit narratological treatise, Brooks argues that the individual death (or the promise of the individual end) has increasingly assumed a privileged position as point of narrative closure: 'Freud's essay may offer a model suggestive of how narrative both seeks and delays its end. In particular, his concept of repetition seems fully pertinent, since repetition of all sorts is the very stuff of literary meanings, the basis of our creative perception of relation and interconnection, the means by which we compare and combine in significant patterns and sequences, and thus overcome the meaninglessness of pure contiguity. In the narrative text, repetition constitutes a return, a calling-back, or a turning-back, which enables us to perceive similarity in difference, consequence in contiguity, metaphor in metonymy.' Peter Brooks, 'Repetition, repression, and return: *Great expectations* and the study of plot', NLH (Spring 1980), p. 512.

This perspective also allows one to sort out linguistic levels, to 'master' the game by distinguishing the figurative from the literal, metaphorical execution from 'real' execution. As I will argue later, the various execution threats which pepper *Alice* constitute threats to impose this kind of closure – although, significantly, the executions are all deferred, thus, defeating Alice's (and our) attempt to master the meaning of these events.

38 Note Derrida's identification of Hegel's need to master play only by excluding it in 'From restricted to general economy: a Hegelianism without reserve'. *Writing and*

138

NOTES TO PAGES 63–78

difference, p. 260.

39 In this context, it is interesting to note an important necessity governing the Hegelian 'Wise Man': he must be an atheist. On the other hand, as Kojève argues, Plato is bound to accept God because to deny the possibility of the 'Wise Man' is to transform philosophy into theology. Kojève, p. 91.

40 This is known as 'imperialist nostalgia': as Renato Rosaldo defines it, 'imperialist nostalgia' is the touchingly overpowering sense of loss one feels for the passing of a traditional way of life when one has been implicated in its demise. Renato Rosaldo, 'Imperialist nostalgia', *Representations* (Spring 1989), pp. 107–22.

41 Edward Said has usefully pointed to the important implications of this kind of knowledge of the exotic as a kind of 'framing' or 'corralling': to enclose it, to delimit its boundaries, is to 'domesticate' it to an extent, to make it available for the person doing the framing. 'Like Walter Scott's Saracens, the European representation of the Muslim, Ottoman, or Arab was always a way of controlling the redoubtable Orient, and to a certain extent the same is true of the methods of contemporary learned Orientalists, whose subject is not so much the East itself as the East made known, and therefore less fearsome, to the Western reading public.' Said, p. 60.

42 The oysters seduced by the Walrus in *Through the looking-glass* are the best Carrollian examples of creatures with whom one discourses serving ultimately as meals.

43 Nina Auerbach has observed this about the book. She argues that Dinah the cat functions as the 'personification of Alice's own subtly cannibalistic hunger'. Nina Auerbach, 'Alice and Wonderland: A curious child', *Victorian studies*, 17 (1973), p. 36.

44 One might speculate on a possible ethical motive for Carroll's famous antivivisectionism: an attempt to preserve the 'otherness' of the other, to keep it safe from appropriation for purely human purposes.

45 Compare Dr. Johnson's anti-platonic definition of juristic truth: 'Sir, you [Boswell the barrister] do not know it [the legal case he is arguing] to be good or bad till the Judge determines it. I have said that you are to state facts fairly; so that your thinking, or what you call knowing, a cause to be bad, must be from reasoning, must be from your supposing your arguments to be weak and inconclusive. But, Sir, that is not enough. An argument which does not convince yourself, may convince the Judge to whom you urge it; and if it does convince him, why, then, Sir, you are wrong, and he is right.' James Boswell, *Life of Johnson*, ed. R. W. Chapman (New York: Oxford University Press, 1980), p. 388.

Chapter 3

1 'In fact, one can assume that ethnology could have been born as a science only at the moment when a decentering had come about: at the moment when European culture – and, in consequence, the history of metaphysics and of its concepts – had been dislocated, driven from its locus, and forced to stop considering itself as the culture of reference.' *Writing and difference*, p. 282.

2 Andrew Lang, *Myth, ritual, and religion* (New York: AMS Press, 1906); Freud, *Totem and taboo*.

3 In *The empire's old clothes*, Ariel Dorfman discusses how North American and European cultural exports (specifically, *Babar* and Disney movies) implicitly assimilate for their readers the 'stages' which lead countries from political 'underdevelopment' to political 'development' to those through which children must pass on their way to adulthood. 'The stage of colonial penetration, the stages in which the native assumes Western norms as his models, are felt by the reader to be the stages of his own socialization.' Ariel Dorfman, *The empire's old clothes* (New York: Pantheon, 1983), p. 44.

4 Joseph Conrad, *Heart of darkness* (New York: Norton, 1971), p. 5.

5 Thus, Derrida quotes selectively from Freud's little known work 'Note on the Mystic Writing Pad' (1925) to argue that the Pad offers Freud a model for conceptualizing the contradictory structure of psychic life: its perpetually renewable innocence and its capacity for infinite retention. 'A double system contained in a single differentiated apparatus: a perpetually available innocence and an infinite reserve of traces have at last been reconciled by the "small contrivance placed some time ago upon the market under the name of the Mystic Writing-Pad"'. *Writing and difference*, p. 223.

6 H. Rider Haggard, *She* (London: Longmans, Green & Co., 1921).

7 See Morse Peckham on evolutionary optimism and the pessimistic theories of cultural regression current at this time. Morse Peckham, *Victorian revolutionaries* (New York: George Braziller, 1970), p. 191. Peckham's book also contains a useful discussion of Tylor's central role in having Evolutionary Anthropology shed its innocence of the exercise of power in order to become a legitimate science: the 'final step' along this road, according to Peckham, is to put knowledge in the service of power by acquiring the ability to 'manipulate its subject matter' and 'manage social behavior'. Peckham, p. 204.

8 For a late twentieth-century version of something like this thesis, see Martin Bernal, *Black Athena: the Afroasiatic roots of classical civilization*, vol. 1 (New Brunswick, NJ: Rutgers University Press, 1988). In *The world's desire* (1890), a romance which he wrote in collaboration with Andrew Lang, Haggard maroons Ulysses in ancient Egypt where he encounters the 'world's desire' – an idealized version of Helen of Troy. H. Rider Haggard and Andrew Lang, *The world's desire* (London: Longmans, Green and Co., 1890).

9 J. W. Burrow, p. 240.

10 According to his father's letter, Leo 'supplanted' his Greek mother (*She*, p. 26). Likewise, the philological analysis of his name (Tisisthenes: Vindex: DeVincey: Vincey) suggests an hereditary imperative of vengeance against matriarchy. As the text makes explicit, the hereditary duty of revenge was 'embalmed in an English family name'. *She*, p. 3. For a reading of this novel which discusses Haggard's triple obsession with Egypt, spiritualism, and the New Woman, see Sandra M. Gilbert, 'Rider Haggard's heart of darkness', *Partisan review*, 50/3 (1983), pp. 444-53.

11 Although he is at pains to exempt Conrad, in general, from the charge of 'psychologization' of the quintessentially 'political' experience of imperialism, Fredric Jameson nevertheless strongly implies that Conrad falls into this ideological trap in *Lord Jim*. And, we would have to add, given the narrative parallels between *Lord Jim* and *Heart of darkness* and Jameson's own premises – his intention of placing Conrad within an historical moment in capitalist society in which rationalization and reification had progressed to the point where the 'psychological novel' develops as a symptom of reified consciousness – in *Heart of darkness*. While Jameson lauds *Nostromo* as the 'interrogation of a hole in time' which is, in essence, a 'meditation on History', he argues that *Lord Jim* 'remains stubbornly deflected onto the problematic of the individual act, and puts over and over again to itself questions that cannot be answered. . . The existential investigation has been rigorously prosecuted, but ends up in neither truth nor metaphysics, but in philosophical paradox.' Fredric Jameson, *The political unconscious: narrative as a socially symbolic act* (Ithaca, NY: Cornell University Press, 1981), p. 264.

12 McClure argues that 'incorporation' in this book is always a form of cannibalism. John A. McClure, *Kipling and Conrad: the colonial fiction* (Cambridge, Ma.: Harvard University Press, 1981), p. 142.

13 As the Russian reveals to Marlow: 'He could be very terrible. You can't judge Mr. Kurtz as you would an ordinary man. No, no, not Now – just to give you an idea – I don't mind telling you, he wanted to shoot me too one day – but I don't judge him.' *Heart of darkness*, p. 57.

14 'To Conrad the end of action was to be found in the preservation of the individual's identity and self-consciousness.' Sandison, p. 109.

15 Jameson discusses Conrad's 'existentializing metaphysics' as a 'containment strategy'. Jameson, p. 216.
16 See Martin Wiener's argument that Hardy was popularly treated as the most influential English spokesman for an anti-capitalist nostalgia for the rural at the turn of the century. Martin J. Wiener, *English culture and the decline of the industrial spirit, 1850–1980* (Cambridge: Cambridge University Press, 1981), p. 52.
17 Merryn and Raymond Williams discuss Hardy's acute awareness of the problems of assimilation caused by the increasing social mobility of members of the two 'classes' out of which he came: the rural working folk and the rural 'intermediate' class, the class of Hardy's father. Merryn and Raymond Williams, 'Hardy and social class', *Thomas Hardy: the writer and his background*, ed. Norman Page (New York: St. Martin's, 1980), p. 31.
18 Thomas Hardy, *The life and work of Thomas Hardy*, ed. Michael Millgate (Athens, Ga.: University of Georgia Press, 1985), p. 241.
19 Edward Clodd, *The childhood of the world: a simple account of man's origin and early history* (1878; New York: Macmillan, 1914). See the Preface to the First Edition: 'Thanks to the patient and careful researches of men of science, the way is rapidly becoming clearer for tracing the steps by which, at evervarying rates of progress, the leading races have advanced from savagery to civilization, and for thus giving a completeness to the history of mankind which the assumptions of an arbitrary chronology would render impossible.' Clodd, pp. v-vi.
20 As Irving Howe claims: 'The kind of work he [Jude] does, restoring old churches, pertains to the traditional English past, but the way he does it, hiring himself out for wages, points to the future.' Irving Howe, 'A distinctively modern novel', *Thomas Hardy, Jude the obscure*, ed. Norman Page (New York: Norton, 1978), p. 399.
21 Raymond Williams, *The country and the city* (New York: Oxford University Press, 1973), p. 198.
22 Cf. Freud's description of his grandson who constructed a simple game with a spool and thread to attempt to 'master' his feelings of frustration at being separated from his mother. Sigmund Freud, *Beyond the pleasure principle*, trans. James Strachey (New York: Norton, 1961), p. 9. However, the question of 'mastery' in this Freudian text is a very complex one. In some respects, Freud's grandson's game represents a capitulation to the fact that he can never 'master' the emotions engendered by this separation, indeed, that 'mastery' under the circumstances of what is a universal experience of loss makes no theoretical sense. This interpretation would be consistent with one of the Freudian 'voices' in *Beyond the pleasure principle*: the 'voice' which asserts 'the aim of all life is death'. On this view of the matter, life is a 'disease' leading, through an indeterminate number of 'detours', to death; 'health' or 'mastery' is a metaphysical illusion or 'disease of language'. One might call this interpretation a 'Hardyan' reading of Freud.
23 Thomas Hardy, *Jude the obscure*, ed. Irving Howe (Boston: Houghton Mifflin, 1965), p. 13. The first edition of *Jude the obscure* was published in 1895. The volume cited here is the text of the 'Wessex Edition', first released in 1912.
24 The railroad came to Dorchester when Hardy was seven years old. R. J. White, *Thomas Hardy and history* (New York: Harper and Row, 1974), p. 53.
25 Herbert Spencer, *First principles* (New York: A. L. Burt, 1880), p. 241.
26 While it may be convenient to speak here as if Jude experiences historical repetition as re-experiencing of primal trauma, this novel problematizes any attempt to locate a 'primal scene'. In psychological terms, the primal scene can never be re-experienced because it is itself constructed of memories inscribed in different spheres of meaning and conjoined in the unconscious. (See Laplanche, pp. 38-47.) A more accurate way of conceptualizing Jude's 'repetitive' plot would be to see it as 'originary deferral'. As Derrida notes in reference to Freud's *Beyond the pleasure principle*: 'No doubt life protects itself by repetition, trace, *différance* (deferral). But we must be wary of this formulation:

there is no life present *at first* which would *then* come to protect, postpone, or reserve itself in *différance*. The latter constitutes the essence of life. Or rather: as *différance* is not an essence, as it is not anything, it is *not* life, if Being is determined as *ousia*, presence, essence/existence, substance or subject. Life must be thought of as trace before Being may be determined as presence. This is the only condition on which we can say that life is death, that repetition and the beyond of the pleasure principle are native and congenital to that which they transgress.' *Writing and difference*, p. 203. Jude's 'origin' is a rupture, as his 'original desire' for Christminster is already secondary, already substitutive, already someone else's – Phillotson's, in fact. What is remarkable about this novel is the way in which it seems to posit a level of the 'natural', the 'instinctual', the 'primary', but then threatens this foundation by unmasking it as 'cultural', 'derivative,' 'secondary'. Consequently, one of the major critical questions about this book – what, fundamentally, does Sue Bridehead want out of life? – is unanswerable, because the origin of her desires is lost in the play of mirroring desires without a point of origination. Moreover, although Arabella seems at first to be associated with an unproblematic 'instinctual', her 'artfulness' and manipulative behaviour render her character anomalous in much the same way.

27 J. Hillis Miller, *Thomas Hardy: distance and desire* (Cambridge, Ma.: Harvard University Press, 1970), p. 18.

28 'The fresh harrow-lines seemed to stretch like the channellings in a piece of new corduroy, lending a meanly utilitarian air to the expanse, taking away its gradations, and depriving it of all history beyond that of the few recent months, though to every clod and stone there really attached associations enough and to spare – echoes of songs from ancient harvest-days, of spoken words, and of sturdy deeds. Every inch of ground had been the site, first or last, of energy, gaiety, horse-play, bickerings, weariness. Groups of gleaners had squatted in the sun on every square yard. Love matches that had populated the adjoining hamlet had been made up there between reaping and carrying. Under the hedge which divided the field from a distant plantation girls had given themselves to lovers who would not turn their heads to look at them by the next harvest; and in that ancient cornfield many a man had made love-promises to a woman at whose voice he had trembled by the next seed-time after fulfilling them in the church adjoining.' *Jude*, p. 13.

29 Gillian Beer argues that Hardy was oppressed by what Darwin celebrated: 'history prolonged beyond consciousness'. Gillian Beer, *Darwin's plots* (Boston: Routledge, 1983), p. 252.

30 Of course, Pater was himself a 'Christminster' don, albeit an unusual one.

31 Note the significant metaphors here: 'town life' as a 'book', Christminster's self-division into 'town' and 'gown'.

32 Hardy was always keenly aware of the fact that any attempt at 'restoration' of an historical monument (i.e. 'recovery' of the historical past) is beset by a number of problems, among them the important fact that the effacement of the past also has a very long history. Hardy, 'Memories of Church Restoration', *Life and art* (New York: Greenberg, 1925), p. 102.

33 Such a configuration, by the way, is an archetypal 'colonial' situation: the 'native' educated and groomed in the imperial 'metropolis' often poses the gravest political threat to the continuation of colonial rule, although the very fact that the 'native' could become 'educated' is celebrated by imperialists as the most remarkable achievement of empire. See Mannoni, pp. 132–41.

34 Miller has noted the way in which Hardy erects necessary barriers between Jude and Sue in order to establish the distance which feeds desire. Miller, p. 166.

35 Miller notes that Hardy's 'eternal recurrence' doctrine is but one of many such formulated in the nineteenth century. While Nietzsche's is, perhaps, best known, Arnold, de Quincey, and Yeats also promulgated such doctrines. Miller, p. 231. 'Far

from forgetting themselves or being forgotten by dying, Hardy's characters enter in death a realm in which every occurrence is doomed to re-enact itself eternally, in an endless failure to escape from itself.' Miller, pp. 230-1.

Because of the striking parallels between Hardy's work and Nietzsche's, it can be distressing to discover that Hardy seems to have had little respect for Nietzsche's ideas. Identifying Nietzsche as a 'moral Darwinian', he shared the view of him common to English intellectuals at the beginning of World War I. As Eugene Williamson argues, Hardy feared the 'naturalistic morality' which he associated with Nietzsche, and later interpreted the events of August 1914 as a 'confirmation of his fears about the result of "masterfulness" as a principle in international affairs'. Eugene Williamson, 'Thomas Hardy and Friedrich Nietzsche: the reasons', *Comparative literature studies*, 15/4 (December 1978), pp. 405-7. However, Hardy is notorious for his ill-treatment of his intellectual influences and contemporaries, although he is hardly alone among European intellectuals in mistakenly identifying 'will-to-power' and 'masterfulness'.

36 Friedrich Nietzsche, *The will to power*, trans. Walter Kaufmann, ed. W. Kaufmann and R. J. Hollingdale (New York: Vintage, 1967), p. 35.

Postscript

1 See Thornton. For a defence of Cobdenite anti-imperialism, see O. Macdonagh, 'The anti-imperialism of free trade', *EconHR*, 14 (1962), pp. 489-501.

2 Sir Charles W. Dilke, *Greater Britain* (London: Macmillan, 1868). James Anthony Froude, *Oceana* (New York: Scribner, 1886). J. R. Seeley, *The expansion of England* (London: Macmillan, 1888).

3 Olive Schreiner's *Trooper Peter Halket of Mashonaland* (London: Fisher Unwin, 1897) presents a believably grotesque vision of Rhodes.

4 See William Strauss, *Joseph Chamberlain and the theory of imperialism* (Washington, DC: American Council on Public Affairs, 1942).

5 Thomas Malthus, *An essay on the principle of population* (London: J. M. Dent, 1973). David Ricardo, *Principles of political economy and taxation* (London: Murray, 1819). Karl Marx, *Capital: a critique of political economy*, vol. I, ed. Frederick Engels, trans. Samuel Moore and Edward Aveling (New York: International, 1967). Patrick Brantlinger, *Rule of darkness: British literature and imperialism, 1830-1914* (Ithaca, NY: Cornell University Press, 1988), pp. 109-34.

6 J. A. Hobson, *Imperialism: a study* (London: George Allen and Unwin, 1938), p. 51.

7 See Hobson's critique of the 'imperial federation' scheme. Hobson, pp. 328-55.

8 Rudolf Hilferding, *Finance capital*, ed. Tom Bottomore, trans. Morris Watnick and Sam Gordon (Boston: Routledge and Kegan Paul, 1981). V. I. Lenin, *Imperialism, the highest stage of capitalism, collected works*, Vol. 22 (London: Lawrence and Wishart, N.D.), pp. 185-304. Rosa Luxemburg, *The accumulation of capital – an anti-critique*, trans. anonymous (New York and London: Monthly Review Pr., 1972).

9 Joseph Schumpeter, *Imperialism*, trans. Heinz Norden (New York: Meridian, 1955).

10 Ronald Robinson and John Gallagher, *Africa and the Victorians* (New York: St. Martin's, 1961), p. 21.

11 Joseph Conrad, *Nostromo* (New York: NAL, 1960), p. 98.

Further reading

The listing below is divided into sections that correspond to the main chapters of this book. In addition, I have included under the heading 'Further reading on the general topic' some recent texts which I consider indispensable. To avoid repetitiousness, I have not listed 'primary' works here. References to them can be found in the notes.

Further reading on the general topic

Babha, Homi K., 'The other question: difference, discrimination, and the discourse of colonialism'. eds. F. Barker, P. Hulme, M. Iversen, and D. Loxley, *Literature, politics, and theory: papers from the Essex conference, 1976-84*. (London and New York: Methuen, 1986), pp. 148-72. Possibly the most influential of Babha's essays, 'The other question' offers his definition of 'colonial discourse' as an 'apparatus' for the exercise of power/knowledge.

Brantlinger, Patrick, *Rule of darkness: British literature and imperialism, 1830-1914* (Ithaca and London: Cornell University Press, 1988). A comprehensive study which argues for the cultural centrality (in Victorian Britain) of the imperial constructions of the culturally alien. Brantlinger's bibliography of Victorian sources is the most useful one available on this topic.

Fanon, Frantz, *Black skins, white masks*, trans. Charles Lam Markmann (New York: Grove Press, 1967). A very influential study of the impact of European imperialism on the colonized by an Algerian who, although trained in psychoanalysis, restores the 'political' context for reading the 'psychology' of imperial rule. See especially his critique of Mannoni, 'The so-called dependency complex of colonized peoples', pp. 83-108.

Green, Martin, *Dreams of adventure, deeds of empire* (New York: Basic, 1979). Green offers a reading of British literary history which emphasizes the historical importance of a gradually evolving disjunction between the values of an 'aristo-military caste' (which provides the cultural impetus for the development of the genre of 'adventure' literature) and a 'bourgeois caste' (which spurs the growth of the 'domestic' novel).

Imperialism and popular culture. ed. John M. MacKenzie (Manchester: Manchester University Press, 1986). A useful collection of historical articles on colonialism's appearance in the popular cultural forms of nineteenth and twentieth

century Britain. For a consideration of the impact of empire on children, see
Imperialism and juvenile literature, ed. Jeffrey Richards (Manchester: Manchester
University Press, 1989).

Mannoni, Octave, *Prospero and Caliban*. trans. Pamela Powesland (New York:
Praeger, 1964). The first substantial 'psychoanalytically-informed' treatment
of the relationship of colonizer to colonized.

'Race', writing, and difference. ed. Henry Louis Gates, Jr. (Chicago and London:
University of Chicago Press, 1986). An indispensable collection of recent
writings on race and the discourse of colonialism. The essays by Edward Said,
Abdul R. JanMohamed, Mary Louise Pratt, Homi K. Babha, Patrick Brantlinger
and Gayatri Chakravorty Spivak are especially useful. In fact, Spivak's essay
'Three women's texts and a critique of imperialism' (pp. 262-80) offers a
reading of *Jane Eyre* which points towards the kind of rereading of Victorian
literary history which this book has attempted.

Spivak, Gayatri Chakravorty *In other worlds: essays in cultural politics* (New York and
London: Routledge, 1988). A collection of essays which map for the first time
some of the interesting theoretical intersections of post-structuralism,
feminism, and 'colonial discourse' theory.

Chapter 1

Blake, Robert, *Disraeli* (London: Eyre and Spottiswoode, 1966). This provides the
most useful reading of Disraeli's literary career in the context of his political
career. For a brief but lively recent biography, see Richard W. Davis, *Disraeli*
(Boston: Little Brown, 1976). Sarah Bradford, *Disraeli* (New York: Stein and
Day, 1983) offers a more psychologically penetrating look at Disraeli's life,
but without the detail or helpful bibliography that Blake provides.

Burke, Edmund, *Reflections on the revolution in France* (London: Penguin, 1979). A
singular articulation of what would become the 'conservative' position
against revolution, this book had an enormous influence on generations of
'conservative' social theorists including Disraeli.

Derrida, Jacques, *Of grammatology*. trans. Gayatri Chakravorty Spivak (Baltimore:
Johns Hopkins, 1976). This work contains Derrida's most comprehensive
discussion of the 'logic' of the 'supplement'. However, *Writing and difference*,
Margins of philosophy, and *Disseminations* are also rich sources for a study pursued
along these lines.

Levine, Richard A., *Benjamin Disraeli* (New York: Twayne, 1968). Still the most
interesting general critical analysis of Disraeli's novels available, although its
critical terminology is a bit outdated now. A first-rate study of Disraeli's novels
has yet to be written. See also Daniel R. Schwarz, *Disraeli's fiction* (London:
Macmillan, 1979).

Mousa, Suleiman, T. E. *Lawrence: an Arab view* (New York and London: Oxford
University Press, 1966). The work which raises the most disturbing questions
about the historical accuracy of T. E. Lawrence's account of his own role in

the Arab rebellion against the Ottoman Empire.

Nietzsche, Friedrich, *Beyond good and evil*, trans. Walter Kaufmann (New York: Vintage, 1966). A 'post-structuralist' writer before there was such a thing as post-structuralism, Nietzsche offers, among his many riches, a rigorous exploration of the inevitably 'political' (i.e. contestatory) field of both psyche and culture. This book focuses on the genealogy of European value structures, locating the responsibility for defining value in the historical accident of political ascendency of a particular class. Thus, Nietzsche's writings are thoroughly anti-foundationalist in tendency, and he is one of the first prominent European intellectuals of the nineteenth century to seriously consider the implications of a philosophical and moral relativism that is one of the 'domestic' cultural after-effects of nineteenth-century imperialism. See his *The will to power*, trans. Walter Kaufmann, ed. W. Kaufmann and R. J. Hollingdale (New York: Vintage, 1967), p. 35 for his exposition of the 'Eternal Recurrence'.

Said, Edward, *Orientalism* (New York: Vintage, 1979). Arguably the book which initiated the post-structuralist re-framing of colonialism and colonialist discourse, Said's *Orientalism* was the first major work to examine modern European imperialism as an historical exercise in what Foucault called 'power/knowledge'. Said's twin claims – that 'orientalist' discourse posited a factitiously unitary referent, the 'Orient', as its object of study and then offered itself as the chief means by which this 'fallen Orient' could be redemptively reclaimed for the 'present' through the mediation of Western power – opened up a new and now dominant direction in the study of imperialism and culture.

Sandison, Alan, *The wheel of empire* (New York: St. Martin's, 1967). A very influential study with continuing relevance, this work offers thoughtful analyses of both Conrad and Kipling as well as a discussion of what Sandison calls Hegel's 'moral imperialism'.

Stocking, Jr., George, *Victorian anthropology* (New York: Macmillan, 1987). By far the most comprehensive and solidly researched treatment of the development of the new 'science' of anthropology and 'racial' theory in nineteenth-century Britain.

Chapter 2

Burrow, J. W., *Evolution and society: a study in Victorian social theory* (Cambridge: Cambridge University Press, 1966). A wryly thoughtful treatment of Victorian social theory, it is an effective complement to Stocking's *Victorian anthropology*.

Cobden, Richard, *The political writings of Richard Cobden*, vol. I (London: Fisher Unwin, 1903; reprinted New York: Kraus, 1969). This work contains the classic defence of 'free trade' by the leader of the Manchester School.

Hegel, G. W. F., *The phenomenology of mind*, trans. J. B. Baillie (New York: Harper and Row, 1967). An indispensable classic, Hegel's *Phenomenology* presents the act of 'knowing' as an act of appropriation, a familiarizing or domestication of the alien. Moreover, his discussion of the interdependency of 'master' and 'slave' was a widely influential one in nineteenth-century Europe. His prose can be a bit forbidding, however, to the uninitiated. For a very helpful introduction, see Alexandre Kojève, *Introduction to the reading of Hegel*, assembled by Raymond Queneau, ed. Allan Bloom, trans. James H. Nichols, Jr. (New York: Basic, 1969).

Huizinga, J., *Homo ludens*, trans. anonymous (London: Routledge and Kegan Paul, 1949). Still the best overall discussion of the function of the 'ludic' in Western culture, it should be read in conjunction with Jacques Ehrmann's deconstruction of its central assumption that play and work are necessarily and universally opposed. See Jacques Ehrmann, 'Homo ludens revisited', *Yale French studies*, 41 (1968). Kathleen Blake, *Play, games, and sport: the literary works of Lewis Carroll* (Ithaca: Cornell University Press, 1974) makes effective use of both writers in her analysis of Carroll's literary works.

Livingstone, David, *Dr. Livingstone's Cambridge lectures* (Cambridge: Deighton, Bell and Co., 1858). This volume contains Dr Livingstone's public musings on the future of Africa. Livingstone argues both that Africa needs to be redeemed (religiously and economically) and that it needs to be protected from the depradations of European adventurers and Arab slave-traders.

Mason, Philip, *Kipling: the glass, the shadow, and the fire* (New York: Harper and Row, 1975). The most useful biography of Kipling available currently.

Rorty, Richard, *Philosophy and the mirror of nature* (Princeton, NJ: Princeton University Press, 1979). Inspired by Deweyan pragmatism and Derridean deconstruction, Rorty's work questions the claims of analytic philosophy to offer a metalanguage for epistemology. His notion of 'incommensurable discourses' has important analogues in a wide variety of fields, including cultural interpretation and Worffian linguistics.

Wittgenstein, Ludwig, *Philosophical investigations I*, trans. G. E. M. Anscombe (New York and London: Macmillan, 1958). The essential starting point for any analysis of social order in terms of 'language games'.

Chapter 3

Beer, Gillian, *Darwin's plots* (Boston: Routledge, 1983). An excellent study of the impact of larger Darwinian themes on Victorian literature, this book contains, among other things, some very useful and wide-ranging readings of Eliot and Hardy.

Dorfman, Ariel, *The empire's old clothes* (New York: Pantheon, 1983). These essays offer an interesting critical discussion of European and American cultural imperialism in the twentieth century. Dorfman argues that European and American popular cultural exports perform an implicitly imperial political function in the late twentieth century: no longer able to teach the old lesson about the inherent racial superiority of Europe, these cultural productions instead repeat the old lesson in a new guise by teaching the formerly colonized that they are 'underdeveloped' in economic, political, and cultural terms.

Hardy, Thomas, *The life and work of Thomas Hardy*, ed. Michael Millgate (Athens, Ga.: University of Georgia Press, 1985). This work reveals Hardy at work constructing the myth of Thomas Hardy. It should be read 'against' a good contemporary biography such as Michael Millgate's *Thomas Hardy* (London and New York: Oxford University Press, 1982).

Jameson, Fredric, *The political unconscious: narrative as a socially symbolic act* (Ithaca, NY: Cornell University Press, 1981). Jameson presents a very ambitious and influential theory of cultural production and reproduction by 'rereading' the pschoanalytically-informed post-structuralist contestation of unitary subjectivity in terms that restore its 'political' rather than 'individual' constitution. Along the way, Jameson offers some excellent readings of, among other writers, Gissing and Conrad.

McClure, John A., *Kipling and Conrad: the colonial fiction* (Cambridge, Ma.: Harvard University Press, 1981). An ambitious study which remains faithful to its goal of tracking both writers' literary preoccupations with empire to their roots in biographical experience as imperial subjects and masters.

Index